Storytime with Robert

Robert A. Johnson Tells his Favorite Stories and Myths

Compiled and Edited
by Nonnie Cullipher

CHIRON PUBLICATIONS • ASHEVILLE, NORTH CAROLINA

www.ChironPublications.com

Interior and cover design by Danijela Mijailovic
Copyright of front cover image: Russ Hopkins. Used with permission.
Printed primarily in the United States of America.

ISBN 978-1-63051-862-2 paperback
ISBN 978-1-63051-863-9 hardcover
ISBN 978-1-63051-864-6 electronic
ISBN 978-1-63051-865-3 limited edition paperback

Library of Congress Cataloging-in-Publication Data

Names: Johnson, Robert A., 1921-2018. | Cullipher, Nonnie, compiler, editor.
Title: Storytime with Robert : Robert A. Johnson tells his favorite stories and myths / complied and edited by Nonnie Cullipher.
Description: Asheville, North Carolina : Chiron Publications, [2020] | Summary: "Robert A. Johnson was more than an international best-selling author of fifteen books, brilliant and influential Jungian analyst, and acclaimed international lecturer; he was a master storyteller. This collection is transcribed from Robert's own tellings throughout the years. Robert told these stories, his favorites, to an appreciative and revering community each night at Journey into Wholeness events from 1981 to 2001. Robert collected several of these stories in his beloved India, but the book includes stories and myths from Chinese, Native American, Mexican, and European traditions. Each story is introduced by a colleague, mentee, or friend whose life was profoundly changed by the presence and teachings of this wise and other-wordly sage. Robert taught us we could enjoy a myth or a story as a child would, or we could listen more carefully to discover a roadmap for our own inner work. Magical, humorous, tragic, enigmatic, these stories illustrate Robert's capacity to speak to the delights and adversities of the human experience, and to our collective quest to become our most conscious and authentic selves"— Provided by publisher.
Identifiers: LCCN 2020034982 (print) | LCCN 2020034983 (ebook) | ISBN 9781630518622 (paperback) | ISBN 9781630518639 (hardcover) | ISBN 9781630518646 (ebook)
Subjects: LCSH: Tales. | Folklore. | Storytelling.
Classification: LCC GR76 .S77 2020 (print) | LCC GR76 (ebook) | DDC 398.2—dc23
LC record available at https://lccn.loc.gov/2020034982
LC ebook record available at https://lccn.loc.gov/2020034983

Acknowledgements

This book is a collaborative effort, and it could not have been written without the help of many talented, patient, and supportive people.

Stephen Rapp, my sound engineer, and Ian Chrisafis, my transcriptionist, were with me from the beginning, before I knew if this project would make it out into the world. Thank you for your diligence and patience during that initial, scattered time.

Thank you to the team at Chiron Publications for believing there was an audience for this book and for your patience with my many edit requests during the cover design phase. Thank you to the Chiron design team, Avi Lane, Phil Cousineau, Amanda Focke, Megan Kidwell, Christine Kosiba, Keri Duff Zink, and my daughter, Brittany Gollins, for your discerning eyes and artistic sensibilities.

Many thanks to my daughter, Greta Cullipher, for your editing, formatting skills, and for your patience and flexibility as this project took over the dining room table for months.

To my late husband, Sid, thank you for your love, our family, your life-changing influence, and for introducing me to the Journey Into Wholeness community where I met Robert and where we experienced much growth, family, and inspiration.

While a book of stories told by Robert A. Johnson was sure to appeal to many, it's the addition of the introductions of my contributors that make this book the project I envisioned for twelve years. Your names are all listed in the book, but I want to say again, thank you Murray, Gertrud, Phil, Laurie, Elizabeth, Barry, Rob, Paula, Pete, Virginia, Frank, Pittman, Ruth, and Jim. A special thanks goes to Rob Luke. He is the only contributor I didn't know personally and who did not have a connection to Journey Into Wholeness. He and his family found a home in this country with Robert, and "Bob" was a lifelong father figure to him. It is an honor that you have trusted me with this profound connection and your beautiful story. Each contributor's heartfelt sharing and insights into the stories are what bring this book alive.

And thank you dear Robert for the years of wisdom you shared with us. Your presence was a balm to our spirits, and your stories entertained, puzzled, shocked, inspired, and often left us silent. I continue to work through these stories and others, and I am honored to be the steward of this amazing collection. It is the definitive honor to now share this treasure with others.

Table of Contents

Introduction   1

Chapter 1 The Good Year (Hindu)   7
  Introduced by Murray Stein

Chapter 2 The Miracle of Guadalupe (Mexican)   17
  Introduced by Gertrud Mueller Nelson

Chapter 3 One-Two Man (Paiute)   25
  Introduced by Phil Cousineau

Chapter 4 Savatri and Satchavan (Hindu)   41
  Introduced by Laurie Downs and Elizabeth Rucker

Chapter 5 Cry of the Loon (Inuit)   55
  Introduced by Barry Williams

Chapter 6 The Frog Queen (Hindu)   63
  Introduced by Rob Luke

Chapter 7 The Dame Ragnel (Western)   71
  Introduced by Paula Reeves

Chapter 8 The King and the Sannyasin (Hindu)   77
  Introduced by Pete Williams

Chapter 9 The Woman at the Crossroads (origin unknown) 83
  Introduced by Virginia Apperson

Chapter 10 Heaven's Emissary (Hindu)   91
  Introduced by Frank Roth

Chapter 11 The Rainmaker (Chinese)   97
  Introduced by J. Pittman McGehee

Chapter 12 Transposed Heads (Hindu)   99
  Introduced by Ruth Hill

Chapter 13 The Old Jew (Western)   113
  Introduced by Jim Cullipher

Introduction

This book is a tribute to Robert A. Johnson, an author, Jungian analyst, lecturer, storyteller, philanthropist, and presence who impacted countless lives. His brilliance as a writer is evident in his 15 books, selling over 2.5 million copies worldwide. Robert had an ability to convey Jung's concepts and other complex ideas in a way the reader could feel and identify with—often through the use of story.

Story and Myth were precious to Robert, and were his primary vehicle of teaching.

"First we must learn to think mythologically. Powerful things happen when we touch the thinking which myths, fairy tales, and our own dreams bring to us. The terms and settings of the old myths are strange; they seem archaic and distant to us, but if we listen to them carefully and take them seriously, we begin to hear and to understand."

— Robert A. Johnson, *She: Understanding Feminine Psychology*

Robert knew that stories could be enjoyed with childlike innocence, and also used to do deep, inner work by acting as a diagram of our own souls, illuminating what goes on inside of us at any given time.

He often asked, *"Who is the good king, the servant, the fool, the wise man, and the heavenly maiden in YOU?"*

When asked if stories were real, he would respond with, *"No, they are realer than real."*

According to Robert, modern man believes he is beyond myth and stories because he has a rational mind, but this creates a schism, and story represents the *"feeling function for our illiterate society"* that might bridge that fissure which splits us. I think it was Robert's dominant feeling function that allowed him, and continues to allow him beyond his lifetime, to reach us at such a deeply resonating level.

I met Robert at Journey Into Wholeness, where he lectured, gave workshops, and told bedtime stories to the community for more than 20 of the 30 years the organization existed. Journey Into Wholeness was a southeastern U.S. based organization that offered conferences, vision quests, and workshops on Jungian psychology, Christianity, and the inner and spiritual life. Annette and Jim Cullipher founded this organization in 1977, and Robert became a close friend of theirs, especially Annette, with whom he carried on a twenty-year correspondence and deep friendship. Robert served as grandfather, mentor, analyst, wise old man, and a dear friend to the grateful Journey Into Wholeness community. Just having him in the room grounded the experience of the people as they learned and shared.

I joined the community in its last decade, marrying Sid, the son of Annette and Jim. I immediately began working for the organization, and served as Assistant Director under Sid and then Executive Director for its final six years. My time with Robert was shorter than many other members of the community, but rich and powerful in my spiritual and psychological development. My extroverted feeling nature got some chuckles and raised eyebrows from Robert and this introverted feeling community, but I felt valued, seen, and understood by Robert as the years passed. He was one of the analysts present for my first vision quest experience, which had me terrified and convinced I would be devoured and irrevocably lost to the spirit world if I was open and vulnerable to it.

The morning I was to set out on my solo, he said, *"Nonnie, not everyone needs a vision quest. Some people have been on a vision quest their whole lives."*

I went anyway and returned to this world safely, but I have never forgotten his words that validated my fears and the adversity of my own personal journey.

The stories you'll read in these pages are transcribed from recordings of those precious bedtime stories Robert told us each night at Journey events. I've listened to about 100 tapes to find a sampling of those that I think represent his favorites. Many choices were simple, like "Transposed Heads," which Robert declared *"is the best story I know."* He also said it was a woman's story, and I'd love to hear what readers make of that statement. "The Rainmaker" is short, but profound. Jung declared that if you had any idea at all what that story meant, you would understand what he was trying to teach. "One-Two Man," is one that Robert particularly identified with, and worked deeply in his memoir, *Balancing Heaven and Earth*. There are many Hindu stories from Robert's beloved India—"*where people understand such things far better than we do*"—and many from the Western tradition that Robert felt were vital to understanding the collective history and development of our own culture. A few stories focus on loneliness, as this was the chief cause of suffering for Robert until late in his life.

When Journey closed in 2007, I donated the organization's entire library of recorded lectures and workshops to Jim Hollis and the Jung Society of Houston, except for all of the recordings of Robert's stories and some key lectures about them, which I purchased. I knew there would be an audience for this book of storytellings and that Robert's singularity and impact could be expressed in no better form.

There are introductions to each story written by analysts, authors, and dear friends who worked with Robert and Journey Into Wholeness over the years. The Journey Into Wholeness community received such a gift in that the love and admiration we showed Robert was reciprocated. In a March 1997 letter to Annette Cullipher, Robert illustrates this shared affection and respect, which is why I think we got the very best of him.

"You and Journey mean so much to me! You and the people who congregate around Journey are the best community I have and that is a rare gift in this isolated world. Someone asked Dr. Jung what was the prevailing archetype of our time; he replied with a single word, 'Disintegration.' The most important task we have these days is to discern what needs to go—many aspects of medieval thinking no longer work for us—but keep safe the

things of human companionship and relatedness. Journey does this better than anything of its kind that I know."

This collection is by no means complete, but it represents many of the stories and myths Robert loved best, and those he knew modern people needed the most. A few of these stories were told once or twice a year for almost 20 years, and many of us now tell them too. Some illuminate complex, psychological principles. Several are relational, giving us a map to reach and understand each other in a more meaningful, conscious, and authentic way. One is included for the sole purpose of making us laugh. For his quiet and stately manner, few people had such a rich sense of humor as Robert Johnson. The twinkle in his eye, and the subtle mirth in his voice, fed his admirers as much as his keen understanding of and ability to clarify elusive concepts. One was always present in the other, and that made him a man and teacher like no other.

Robert spoke frequently of the Storyteller caste of India. After decades of storytelling under the banyan tree, one day the wise man would just get up and walk away and the young man who had been sitting and listening would slide, quietly, into the wise man's place, allowing a seamless and natural transition. My hope is that you will enjoy this unique experience to hear again, or for the first time, a very special wise man's stories.

Chapter 1
The Good Year

Introduced by Murray Stein

I remember the scene so well. The setting was the annual Journey Into Wholeness conference at Kanuga Conference Center in Hendersonville, North Carolina. Robert Johnson was about to tell one of his famous bedtime stories. This evening it would be a story from India with the title, "The Good Year." It was springtime and Journey was in full swing. One had the sense that people were getting what they had come for. I had been a speaker at Journey several times before, and had gotten to know Robert quite well. He was a regular at these annual gatherings, and he had a devoted following here. Though deeply introverted, Robert was extremely warm and gracious in this company. One could see clearly that the people loved—actually, "adored" would be the better word—this master storyteller. Everyone referred to him as "Robert," and we all knew immediately who was meant when that name was mentioned. There was only one Robert.

On this evening, the air was redolent with the scents of spring in the woods as people ambled into the lecture hall, sat down, and engaged in quiet conversation while waiting for Robert to take his place at the podium and begin his story for the night. This was a daily event, much anticipated and beloved. The Culliphers, husband and wife, were about, as always, and everyone was happy to be here. Then Robert took his place and silence descended over the room as he looked out over the audience and prepared his opening lines.

Robert told his stories from memory and without notes, and his style and pace were mesmerizing. "The Good Year" was a story I have never forgotten, and to this day I use it in lectures to students and general audiences when I speak about the individuation process in Jungian psychology.

"The Good Year" is a wise story. It tells of a king at midlife who, though he has everything material he could possibly want, feels that "something" important is missing from his life. He is not sure what, but when he hears of a teacher far off at the edge of his kingdom, he decides to search him out and see if he might have an answer to his question. He is not disappointed. Although the path forward is not an easy one, he does follow the instruction of "renunciation" faithfully, and after making a number of major changes in his life does find his way to a new attitude and a feeling of satisfaction. He finds what has been missing.

"The Good Year" is a story of transformation, and it illustrates the archetypal pattern of individuation that moves progressively from ego grandiosity to service of the

Self. It is a pattern that one can also see in the Bible, as I have written about in a work that had its origins at Journey Into Wholeness, The Bible as Dream.

I have thought a lot about the importance of renunciation while working with analysands and guiding students in their training to become Jungian psycho-analysts. We start with a feeling of need and a sense that something is missing, and then we take a risk and go on a journey. This was Jung's condition when he set out on the journey to find his teacher, Philemon. His story is told in The Red Book. *It is a long and difficult journey, often filled with loss and painful choices. It is what we call "the journey to wholeness." What begins with ego inflation goes through a process of separation and integration that results in a living relation to the transcendent.*

Robert knew this pathway, with all its twists and turns, as well as anyone I have ever met. I am grateful that he introduced this wonderful story into my life on that memorable evening at Kanuga.

Murray Stein, Ph.D., is a training and supervising analyst at the International School of Analytical Psychology in Zurich, Switzerland.

Once there was a king. And though he was a young man, he was a very good king. The kingdom prospered, the people were happy, there was peace with the neighboring kingdoms, and everything seemed as good as it could possibly be. The king lived with his beautiful queen, he had a large harem, he had a grand household, he was beloved by his subjects, and everything worked as an old-fashioned kingdom should work. But there was some lack gnawing away inside the young king, and he didn't know what it was.

One day he heard that there was a wise man who lived in the forest at the far end of his kingdom, and that resonated with this insufficiency inside himself.

He said quietly, "I have to go and see that wise man because surely he has something for me."

So, the king set up his retinue, as a king must do when he moves, and it took something like 500 elephants to take his queen, a palanquin, and himself. He took all of his harem, a large part of his army, and he took his cooks and a whole retinue of people. An assembly like this moves very slowly, so it took several days before they reached the forest at the far side of his kingdom. The young king was naturally a humble and respectful man. So, when he got a few hundred yards from where the wise man sat under the banyan tree, he came down from the palanquin on the elephant and he walked, as an honor or a dignity to the wise man.

He came to the old wise man who was sitting under the banyan tree. If ever there was a meeting of opposites, this was it. The king with all of his retinue and the wise man who sat alone with only a loincloth and a begging bowl under the banyan tree. The young king brought his presents, he sat down cross-legged, and he waited a discreet length of time.

He finally said to the old wise man, "I ask that you would teach me."

The old wise man sat there and an unbelievable length of time went by. With the air so charged with meaning and expectation as it was, time seemed to stretch itself out just interminably.

After an endless time, the wise man drew a deep breath and fairly roared forth a single word, "Renunciation!"

Then he then closed his eyes and went into meditation and made it plain that this was the end of the interview.

So the young king, considerably taken aback by all of this, and seeing no further instructions were going to come, got up. He got back on his elephant and they all went back the several days journey to the palace again. He thought very deeply about this new teaching and he thought he understood. He focused his mind on the principle of renunciation, and for a year he reduced the power play, the extravagance, and the glitter of the court. He ate less, he talked less, he dressed more simply, and he reduced his harem. Fewer people came to him and he spent more time alone. Everything in the kingdom was reduced somewhat. At the end of a year, the kingdom was prospering even more than it had before. The people were aware their king had done something of great depth and power and they were grateful, though they didn't understand it that well.

At the end of the year, the young king thought, "I must go see the holy man and find out what else to do."

So, he went with much less of a retinue and only a few elephants were sufficient this time. He took the queen, only the favorites of his harem, a few cooks, and only a few of the soldiers of his army. They made a much quieter entourage this time, making their way through the forest to the other side of the kingdom.

When they came to the old wise man, they found him sitting there just as before. The king walked up to him and sat down gracefully and respectfully and waited a long period of time before he asked the old wise man for further instruction.

The old wise man sat there for that impossible length of time. The kind of time that seems to stretch out until you think you had blundered into infinity.

Finally, he drew a deep breath and shouted a single word, "Renunciation!"

The king, not quite so surprised this time, waited for a while, a seemly length of time, and got up and got on his elephant and went back to his palace. He pared things down much more. He ate much less, he talked very little except on official business, he pared his harem down to a very small size, fewer soldiers were required, fewer cooks were required, the palace took on a quiet dignity it never had before. The kingdom prospered even more. The people of the kingdom didn't know what was going on, but they knew that their young king was doing something very right.

At the end of a year of this, with everything working so well, the king decided that he needed the presence of the holy man again. He went with only a few of his friends this time and they walked. They went to the old holy man and the king seated himself next to him. After a time without end, he asked the holy man for further teaching, for further wisdom.

An unconscionable length of time passed and the holy man suddenly shouted a single word at him again, "Renunciation!"

Now the king was surprised. He didn't know what to do. He went a little distance away and talked with his friends.

"What would further renunciation consist of? How do you renounce more than what I have done?"

Then the king understood that he had to take up residence under a nearby banyan tree and live in much the same austerity as the old holy man lived.

He lived in this manner for a year. Couriers came and went from the palace and all the business the king was required to do was easily dispatched. The kingdom prospered even better than before. A year of this and the king decided he needed instruction again from the old wise man. He walked the short distance over all by himself this time. He sat before the man, he waited that lengthy span of time, and asked for further instruction. He waited an eternity before the wise man spoke again.

Then the wise man fairly roared out a single word, "Renunciation!"

The king was beside himself this time. He had renounced the palace, the harem, the kingdom, what more was there to renounce? So, he went back to his banyan tree and sent away all of his friends except one trusted companion. They devised the most austere life that they could possibly manage. They ate only the berries and fruit that they could find close at hand, they made clothing from the bark of adjacent trees, they drank from a nearby stream, they lived almost without speech and with as little food and as little clothing as possible. The kingdom prospered even more. The king got messages from the palace as necessary, mostly to find out that the kingdom was operating perfectly. The king learned a profound lesson from all this.

At the end of another year, he needed more instruction, as he knew his learning was not complete. He was much reduced in size and a very quiet man. He walked the distance to the wise man, sat forever, and then asked the old man for further instruction. There followed that bit of eternity that is so hard to take when one is as focused as the king was.

The old wise man drew a deep breath and bellowed forth a single word, "Renunciation!"

Then the king knew. He knew that there was only one further renunciation that was possible for a human to make, and that was to renounce his life.

This revelation was the confrontation with his death. There was no doubt in his mind that he would do this, though it was the most awesome moment of his life. He went back to his banyan tree, dismissed his one friend, and vowed that he would neither eat nor drink so that he might make the final austerity that had been prescribed by the holy man. Soon, he was one day from his death.

He said to himself, "This is the fulfillment of the teaching of which I have asked for, and I want only one thing ... I want to go back and see the holy man just one more time before I give up my life in the final renunciation."

He got some native people nearby to carry him because he was very weak, and he had himself put down before the old holy man. This time it was not difficult for him to wait, because he was within one day of that great waiting.

He said, "Holy man, instruct me one degree further before the time of my death."

And the old holy man waited. Suddenly, he took a deep breath and shouted, fairly to frighten the king, two words, "Renounce renunciation!"

The king was enlightened, and a flood of light came over him like a great wave. The king was enlightened, and he saw. So, he called for his servants and he had them take him back to the palace. He ate food and he grew strong. He approached the queen again, and he built his harem back up to full strength. He employed all of his cooks again, and the army was brought back to full strength. He became the greatest king that India had ever known.

Chapter 2
The Miracle of Guadalupe
Introduced by Gertrud Mueller Nelson

It was 1965. I was nursing my second child when my husband came home for lunch, all aglow with stories about a "Union Analyst" who visited Minneapolis monthly. This analyst worked with dreams and spoke of mythology.

I listened to the enthusiasm and curiosity pouring forth, but urged him to see if this person was not really a "Jungian Analyst." The man speaking was a Robert Johnson, from Michigan, and he was indeed a Jungian. I had read much on Jung and had always wanted to meet a genuine "Jungian"!

We would hire a sitter for our little son, but would have to bring our tiny, nursing daughter along to the evening presentation. But the idea that a woman, nursing a baby, might be coming ... well ... this Robert Johnson was very shy and neither could he really handle any extra attendees, we were told. Only an invited four were coming and really that was all Mr. Johnson could handle. Not so easily dissuaded, I decided I could sit in the far back of the room. I could muffle the kid. There was no question that I needed to attend. If a nursing mother was going to freak this man out, maybe he needed a little therapy himself!

My husband and I struck out for the church in Minneapolis where this seminar of four was to take place. Our daughter lay sleeping happily, disguised in an apple box in the back seat. I slid that apple box right under the long table and we placed ourselves at the far end. There really were only six of us (our seventh tucked out of sight). The seminar was everything I had ever wanted to hear and learn. I was totally enchanted. The baby made the occasional muffled squeak, which was easily resolved by sliding her discreetly under my sweater. At a silent moment of deep pondering by all of us, the happy slurping noises of my daughter suddenly revealed her presence. A quizzical, and then suddenly pale, Robert realized what was going on. The seminar was soon drawn to a close.

From that day forward, Robert visited our house each month when he was in town and he became godfather to our next daughter. We went camping together in the deserts of California and Mexico for years to come. For 54 years he was part of the family and a huge agent in our growing and learning. Robert and I spoke together at seminars. In time, I too wrote books on ritual, myth, and fairy tale. In his last year, lying in his hospital bed, bewildered and in another world, he would greet me with delight.

"It's my MOTHER!" he would say as I entered his room. "With beautiful white hair!"

The power of story was nothing new to me. My mother was an ardent and powerful teller of myths, stories of the saints, and fairy tales. Telling stories or reading them to the kids was in turn not only their delight, but my own. When my youngest was "tested for Kindergarten readiness," I was stunned that there was such a test and apprehensive when the testing psychologist called me that night.

"I was impressed," he said, "with her vocabulary and so I asked her my standard questions for children with advanced vocabularies:

"Do your parents read to you?"

"You mean tell stories? Sure! My Papa tells us Piggle-Wiggle stories and Mama tells us Greek Myths."

"What are myths, do you know?"

"Mythology? Well. Um—those are stories that aren't true on the outside. But they ARE true on the inside."

Annika was right. I know that the distinction of levels is one that Robert tried often to impart to his listeners. We make our gravest errors in life when we try to make an archetypal truth literal and alive on an "outside" level—trying to make it real on the wrong plane. And when we fail to assimilate a powerful archetypal truth because we cannot pinch it or measure it or give it a scientific formula, we discard a potent truth that needs to be assimilated within.

I have no idea where Robert found The Miracle of Guadalupe story. Sometimes his very active imagination slid into place and his stories would bloom accordingly. We see that curious division of the feminine/woman, split into Virgin and Whore with the crisis she suffers, trying to integrate her soul into a wholeness, beyond duality. In this story, it is the dark Virgin/Mother who effects that integrity with our heroine. And thus, Robert's listeners were trundled off to bed, further knitting together the opposites to a third and holy resolution.

Gertrud Mueller Nelson is a mother, granny, artist, liturgical, and jewelry designer. She speaks internationally on liturgy, myth, and fairy tales. Of her dozen or so books, two stand out for Jungians: *To Dance with God: Family Ritual and Community Celebration* **(Paulist Press) and** *Here All Dwell Free: Stories to Heal the Wounded Feminine,* **(Doubleday and Paulist Press).**

There was once an old-style convent, a beautiful building. Old, gothic, worn, the very stones themselves spoke of the years and years, the eons of prayer, which had taken place in the convent. Generations of women came and went. There was once a young novice who came to this convent. She was youthful, she was fresh, and she was full of life. She was the perfect novice. The mother superior was so pleased with her as she never did anything wrong. She understood quickly, she walked, hunched over just a bit, on the far side of the hall to indicate her humility, and she worked hard. She did all of the things, great and small, which make up the art of the conventual life. They met often for the offices of the day. First at two in the morning, then at six, then at nine, then at twelve, and so on. Then off to bed.

One morning at six in the morning, she was saying her prayers, and focusing properly as was her duty. By chance, she looked over at the screen which separated the nuns from the main part of the church, and there was a young man who winked at her. He was handsome, young, dark, and fiery. The poor novice lost custody of her eyes and couldn't keep her mind on the prayers of the morning. She was all aflutter, so at the end of the prayers she went away and it took all day to get her composure back again. She came the next morning, and she was in terror. She was not supposed to look at the screen, but she couldn't help it, the very muscles of her neck and head spun around involuntarily. And there he was again. Not only did he wink at her, but he passed her a note. She was unhinged by now. So she took the note into her habit and somehow survived the rest of the offices of the day.

As soon as she was in privacy, she took the note out, one hand reaching and the other hand refusing. She was terribly, terribly torn.

Finally, she read the note, and good Lord, the note said, "Have your valise packed at midnight. Stay by the window. I will bring the ladder, and we will run away."

She was helpless. She was absolutely out of control. She was so happy she didn't know what to do, and she was so terrified she didn't know what to do. She was so guilty she couldn't function, but she was so energized she couldn't keep still.

Midnight came on leaden feet, and she was at the window of her cell. The fiery man arrived with his ladder, hoisted her over his shoulder, and off they went. They had three delicious days, three wonderful, ecstatic days where time seemed to stop. But the time did stop, and at the end of three days, she discovered he was a demon.

He was cruel to her, and he beat her into submission. This went on and on and on. By the end of the year, she was pregnant. He then abandoned her, and left her an absolutely and completely crushed human being. She managed somehow, and the child was born. The only way she could survive and keep her child, could manage at all, was to turn to prostitution. So she lived a miserable life, and just kept her child alive. It absolutely tore her personality to pieces, but she had that dogged one-track mind: just take care of the boy, no matter what the cost. This is how it had to be.

This went on for some time. At this point she had a dreadful illness, and her health and her strength and her beauty, everything of her womanhood, lay in tatters. Finally, after a couple of months, the boy died. This was the end. She had no more strength, she couldn't think, and there was nothing left to do. She had no courage, no hope, and she wanted to die.

One thought went through her mind, and she said, "I want to see my prayer stall one last time before I die."

She went back to the convent. Nobody recognized her, of course, as she looked like an old woman. All her beauty was gone, all hope was gone, no one in a thousand years would have recognized her, though it was only two years' time since she'd left.

Someone came to the side door, and she asked, "Is there any work?"

A nun said, "Yes, we need a chore woman. Come inside. You'll receive your board, your rooming, and one thruppence a week."

So she came in, and they gave her a bucket, a rag, and hot water. They told her to get down and scrub the floor. She scrubbed all day, grateful for something to do, and for some structure in her life. But then came a dreadful moment, because she found that she was about to scrub the floor beneath her old prayer stall, and suddenly it was too much. She couldn't stand it. She collapsed, just a heap of rags on the floor, an utterly defeated human being.

Then, a miracle happened.

The Virgin Mary descended from her pedestal and came to the girl and touched her on the shoulder. She explained that she had come down every day to take the girl's place in the prayer stall. No one even knew that the girl had been gone. The girl couldn't conceive of this, couldn't believe it.

The Virgin Mary said, "Here's your old habit. Put it on and resume your rightful place. No one will know you ever left. You are home."

The girl did this, and it was just as the Virgin Mary had said. She became such a wise and powerful nun, such a good monastic, that she became the Abbess of the convent and brought it to one of its great flowerings in history.

Chapter 3
One-Two Man
Introduced by Phil Cousineau

To read a myth so that it is relevant to modern life requires extraordinary vision, the uncanny ability to take a psychological X-ray of its archetypal imagery. The brilliant Jungian psychotherapist Robert A. Johnson had a seemingly in-born talent for telling a good story, but he also worked exceptionally hard to develop the capacity to detect in his favorite myths, legends, and literature what he called their interior meaning, which enabled him to animate them so that they might stir our imagination.

Of the scores of stories that Robert learned by heart and told over the course of his long life, his retelling of the Native American Indian story of "One-Two Man" reveals him at his most amiable and discerning. His telling of it also finds him at his most self-revealing.

This venerable myth tells of an orphan boy whose father was a powerful warrior and his mother a kind and wise woman. When his father tragically dies and his mother disappears, the boy is raised by his grandmother. One day she challenges him to screw up his courage and dig for his father's bones under the leaves of a nearby oak tree, and then to look underneath them for the ancestral axe of his people.

So far, so familiar, with what appears to be a traditional quest story. What happens next, though, is unexpected and grisly, while remaining well within the borders of the strange logic that rules the mythic realm. The orphan rouses the spirit of his dead father, who instructs him to leave his childish ways behind and move on to learn the ways of the warrior. To do this, the father tells him to perform a strange task: "Take your axe and you go to Granny and tell her to cleave you in two." Of course, as any grandmother would be with such a request, she is mortified. Eventually, she relents and reluctantly splits him in two, from head to toe. Somehow, although the story does not say explicitly how, the orphan boy is able to embark upon a far more dangerous journey. With the help of several wily animal guides, he sets out to rescue his mother from the clutches of a dangerous monster, which he is warned about, but responds, "If I'm killed, alright, but I have to try."

His valiant spirit reflects the essence of the traditional quest, from Gilgamesh to Odysseus, Inanna to Parsifal, Jane Eyre to Moby-Dick, the suggestion that the real journey is the one that the heroine or hero can't not take.

Hence, Robert's remark that over many years of telling the story he became "astonished at the universality." With much aplomb and no little humor, our young hero accomplishes his goal, which was made actually possible, the story suggests, by his being cleaved—doubled—a split that allowed him to transform from boy to man. The One-Two Man.

When I read and listened to the audio recording of this version of the story, I was transported back to the many workshops I was privileged to lead with Robert at various Journey Into Wholeness venues, several Jung Institute seminars, and an Esalen Institute workshop, as well as the numerous scintillating conversations we had together over tea at his homes in Encinitas and San Diego. Often, he reflected on the meaning of various myths and dreams with me, speculating about their inward depths, their "punctum," as the French semiologist Roland Barthes called the point of a photograph, a work of art, a story, or a theory.

For Robert, I believe the archetypal point, if you will, of the One-Two Man story was the divided soul—a theme he explored in such mythic figures as Don Quixote, Faust, and Hamlet, as well as Parsifal, Eros, and Psyche. Many, if not most of us, he taught, are cut in two, severed, or separated from our real selves. Our task is to heal the breach, by taking on the individuation process, or as he once put it beautifully to me, "to step into our own unique destiny."

"If we are cleaved right down the middle," Robert reflects about One-Two Man, "between ego and shadow, personal and collective dimensions of life, we need to do something to bring the two cleaved together—or be torn apart as a tragedy."

For Robert, the cleaving in his own life was a freak accident when he was eleven years old. A runaway car pinned him to a building, resulting in the loss of one of his legs. A terrible misfortune, but, as he often said, what matters is less what happens to us and more our response to it. He spent the rest of his life gleaning meaning from the accident. Often, he said that he did not believe in chance but did believe in what he called "slender threads," recurrent themes, synchronicities on which our destiny turns.

One day, on the deck of his condominium overlooking the glittering Pacific Ocean in Encinitas, California, Robert read out loud to me from the manuscript of his auto-biography, Balancing Heaven and Earth (cowritten with Jerry M. Ruhl). He emphasized a passage in which he casually wrote that he believed he had been "wounded just enough" by the car that fateful day. By this curious phrase, I took him to mean that the accident had intensified his already introverted nature and enabled him to become what anthropologists call a "wounded healer," an autotelic or self-motivated individual who finds a way to heal himself and others. In this way, he consciously chose not to dramatize or sentimentalize the accident—the cleaving—but to numinize it, considering it one of the several "slender threads" that imbued his life with meaning. No wonder Robert identified with the One-Two Man story.

"Caress the details, the divine details," wrote the Russian novelist and critic Vladimir Nabokov in his book of lectures about American literature. For the details are where the gods and the goddesses dwell. Of the two details he focuses upon in the One-Two Man tale in his brief concluding remarks, the first is revealed with pre-ternatural calm, where the orphan boy is cut in two by his own grandmother. The shocking mythic image is, of course,

28

symbolic, and here it pays to recall Jung's own aphorism, "Never say just a symbol."

Instead, we might ask: symbolic of what? What does it mean to be cleaved, cut in half, psychologically, spiritually, physically? And who hasn't wondered how to put the pieces back together again?

The second "divine detail" that fascinated Robert was the very presence of the grandmother. The choice is most certainly not arbitrary. Here it is not just anybody but an orphan's grandmother who does the cutting. As someone who was likewise raised and dearly loved by his grandmother, Robert's interpretation is fascinating. If a child is raised by parents in their twenties and thirties, he says here, she is raised in the world of housekeeping, but if raised by grandparents she is initiated into the realm of the elders, which provides access to the world of folklore and elder wisdom. Often, these youths survive by becoming artists, priests, storytellers, or healers, someone of an interior nature—or become a psychological misfit, a tragedy.

With sudden gravitas in his voice, Robert says, "For somebody who goes through that experience, he has only two choices or options in the world, and there are only two."

Every thinking person is, as it were, cut in two, by the miseries and sorrows of life, and we are, as he says here about One-Two Man, faced with a dilemma: stay severed, separated from our true selves, or find a way to heal ourselves.

To my lights, the cleaving in this many-sided myth is a gift, an introduction to what the ancient Irish called the

Back of Beyond, which is where myth, art, spiritual life, and music reside. All those realms where Robert lived out his days and nights as healer and healed.

Inspired by the One-Two Man story all over again, I went back to a folder of notes I have kept from my many conversations with Robert, and found an intriguing one from June 1995 in which he told me about asking one of his other significant "slender threads," the time he boldly asked his mentor, Dr. Carl Jung, "Are we going to make it?" In my notes I am moved even now how he added parenthetically, "In other words, I was asking Dr. Jung if we would survive as a species."

"If enough people do the inner work," is what Robert told me Jung replied.

By the inner work, he meant healing the rifts in our riven souls, rebalancing our conscious with our un-conscious lives, exploring the sacred dimension through dreams and mythic stories that may lead us to what he fondly called the "Golden World," where we are finally at peace.

I can hear Robert's sonorous voice as he spoke to me about his many cups of tea with Jung in Bollingen, and as I do I am transported back to his home, high on a cliff overlooking the Pacific Ocean, where he would ritually pour Darjeeling tea for us from a beautiful iron kettle, and share with me how he had struggled with loneliness all his life but had been saved by three things: immersing himself in his dreams and the dreams of others, his annual pilgrimages to India, and his intimate conversations with close friends.

I was wonderstruck by his clarion-clear descriptions of how cleaved his life had been, but even more by how unswerving he was with how he used his own ancestral axe to carve out an authentic and selfless life.

Unfailingly, after his ruminations, Robert would pour another cup of tea for us then turn to me and ritually ask, "Have you had any interesting dreams or heard any good stories lately?"

Phil Cousineau is a freelance writer, filmmaker, and mythologist. He has published more than 35 books, including *The Art of Pilgrimage*, and *Coincidence or Destiny*, for which Robert Johnson wrote the Foreword, and more than 25 documentary films. He is the host and cowriter of the PBS and Link TV series, "Global Spirit."

One-Two Man was a boy, and he was also an orphan. He was being raised by Granny, who was very good to him. He and Granny loved each other profoundly, and One-Two Man was well taken care of.

One day in the springtime, when he was ten or eleven years old, he went in to Granny and he said, "Granny, I'm bored, tell me something to do."

So Granny said, "Why don't you go out and dig some roots? Find all the things that grow underneath the ground, potatoes and yams and tubers and the like, and make a big collection." This caught One-Two Man's imagination and off he went with his shovel.

All summer long, One-Two Man dug roots, and he came in several times a day and took Granny by the hand to show her how big the pile of roots was. He dug and he dug and he worked all summer long. In the fall he had an enormous pile of roots, taller than he was and many times his length. One morning in the fall, he went out, and he was going to add to his great pile of roots and, horror of horrors, the roots were all gone. There wasn't one left.

He couldn't believe his eyes, and went dashing in to Granny, "Granny, Granny! The roots are all gone! What's happened? My roots! My roots are gone!"

Granny looked very sober, and she said, "Yes, I know. There's something I've got to tell you, and I've been saving it and I've been waiting and I've been delaying it, but I have to tell you about your mother and your father. This is why the roots are gone.

"Your father was a great warrior, the greatest of all warriors, and no one wielded a spear, or a stone axe, or a bow and arrow better than your father. He had a wonderful wife, your mother, and she was very good and very kind."

Granny was crying by this time, and One-Two Man was no longer thinking about roots because this was much more important.

Granny went on with her story, "Then you were born, and an awful thing happened. There was a medicine man, named Old Stoneshirt, who had taken his shamanic powers and used them evilly, for his own use, instead of for healing. He had gotten so evil and so cold that he had grown around his entire body a shirt of stone, which no bull, no arrow, no axe, no spear could go through. He was absolutely invulnerable, and nobody could kill him or defend themselves against him. With his shamanic powers and his stone shirt he could do anything he wanted, and his power went more and more to his head. One day he decided he wanted your mother. Your father fought him valiantly, but he could do nothing to stop him, and Old Stoneshirt killed your father. He abducted your mother, and he keeps her in the far corner of a cave over on the other side of the valley, where she can never get out and no one can rescue her. The cave is guarded at the entrance by an antelope which has an eye on the end of every hair. No one can get by the antelope, because those eyes are never asleep all at the same time. Worse than this, inside the cave, Old Stoneshirt has two daughters by a marriage from long, long ago, and they are just as malicious as he is. They are armed with magic bows and arrows which never miss their target. So your mother is captive in the back of that old cave, and Stoneshirt lives there, and with this guard there is nothing that anybody can do.

"Your father came last night in his spirit, and he took the pile of roots away, and he said,

'This is good work for a boy, but it is not worthy of my son, who now must be taught the art of warriorhood.'

"So your father took the roots away and said you are not to dig any more roots, because that is boys' work. He said you are to go over to his grave, which is on the north side of that big oak tree in the center of the clearing, and you are to dig at the grave with your hands. Just under the surface, you will find the bones of your father. This will frighten you very much, but you must be brave. You will take the bones of your father and set them aside, and underneath the bones you will find a stone axe, which was given to your father by his father, and in turn by his father, and ahead of that by his father, and for more generations back than anyone can remember. It is now your stone axe, because you are a warrior. This stone axe, which has come down through so many generations, and was your father's, is now to be yours. And when you have the axe, you are to put the bones of your father back in the grave, lie down upon them with the axe in hand, and go to sleep. For four days and four nights, you will sleep, and the spirit of your father will come and instruct you in warriorhood. When you wake up, you will be a full-grown warrior. This is what your father has said."

One-Two Man was absolutely speechless. The boy who, half an hour ago, had all of his focus on gathering roots, now thought very little of roots, and he didn't know what to do. It took several days of One-Two Man moping about and kicking things from here to there until he got up the courage to go to the north side of the old oak tree and begin to dig for his father's bones. Finally, he went, and he set the oak leaves aside, and he dug down just a little ways, and he came to the bones of his father. Then, a pitiful thing happened. He completely lost courage, and he backed up, got some stones, and threw them in fear at the bones of his father. A boy who can't cope with something will probably throw stones of some sort or another. Nobly, his father's spirit did not throw stones back. Finally, One-Two Man stopped his cowardice and his antagonism and his stone throwing, and gingerly and gently picked up the bones of his father, one after the other, and set them aside. There was the ancestral axe, which had come down through so many generations, and which now belonged to One-Two Man. He carefully put the bones back into the grave, covered them over, curled himself up with his stone axe in hand, and went to sleep.

For four days and four nights, he slept, and the spirit of his father came and instructed him on everything that he needed for warriorhood: how to track animals, how to use a bow and arrow, how to use the stone axe, the ways of the forest, the secrets of weather, all the things a warrior must know. At the end of four days, when he woke up, he was full-grown, full-muscled, and had all of the things that he needed: his bow and his arrow and his axe and his shield. He was a real warrior.

The spirit of his father came to him and said, "Now, there is one more thing: take your axe and go to Granny and tell her to cleave you right down the middle, from the very top of your head to the bottom of your two feet. You are to be cut right in two."

One-Two Man was not questioning anything now, so he went and showed himself, in his full strength and his warriorhood, to Granny, who admired him greatly, and was very pleased.

He said, "My father said to give you the axe and that with all of your strength you are to cleave me in two, from the top of my head to the bottom of my feet."

Granny burst into tears, and she said, "I couldn't do such a thing to you, I love you too much! Don't ask me to do such a terrible thing!"

One-Two Man put the stone axe in her hand and said, "My father, your son, said that this is to be done, and you must do it."

Granny was shaken to the core, but she gathered all of her strength together, and in one mighty blow she cut One-Two Man into two pieces, from the top of his head to the bottom of his feet.

One-Two Man immediately announced that he was going to rescue his mother.

"No, no, no, you'll just get yourself killed! Old Stoneshirt can vanquish you, absolutely and for certain. Don't try or you'll find yourself dead in your father's grave as well. A medicine man who uses his powers for evil is absolutely unassailable."

One-Two Man said, "Whether I win or whether I lose, I am going to go and try to free my mother."

One-Two Man, while he was a boy, had made friends with all the animals of the forest and the desert. He called his friends together and showed off his new warrior abilities and his strong body, and they all rejoiced and complimented him.

He then told them the story of Old Stoneshirt, and he said, "I am going to go and rescue my mother."

Bighorn Sheep said, "No, no, no, don't try it. You'll just get yourself killed, and we will be without you."

And Wolf said, "No, there's no chance."

And Coyote said, "No, there's no chance."

And Mouse said, "No, there's no way."

And Rattlesnake said, "No, it's foolhardy. Don't try it."

One-Two Man said, "Alright, I have asked for your advice and you have given it to me, but I am going to do it anyway. If you want to come with me, you can, and if you don't want to, you don't have to."

His animal friends each then said, "Well, if you're going to do it, yes, of course, your friends will come along with you. We will all be killed, but we are companions, and if you are going, we will go."

Bighorn Sheep offered a bowl of water which never ran dry. In that dry, arid country of the Southwest desert, the first requirement for any action was to make sure there was an adequate water supply. Wolf came next, and Wolf never stopped talking. He gave advice until it would make your ears weary. Coyote came, and Coyote was also full of advice, and he talked until one was weary far into the night. Mouse came, and Mouse didn't have anything very tangible to offer, but Mouse was there. Rattlesnake came, and Rattlesnake was absolutely quiet, and was so well-camouflaged on the desert floor that unless you looked very closely, and knew where he was, you wouldn't see him. And so the powwow began. One-Two Man told them that Old Stoneshirt lived in the cave, guarding One-Two Man's mother, with the two sisters with bows and arrows that never missed, and that awful antelope that guarded the mouth of the cave, with an eye at the end of every hair which never slept all at the same time. Wolf was full of ideas, and he spent weeks talking and devising schemes. Coyote was also full of ideas, and he talked for weeks and weeks, until no one's ears could take it anymore.

Mouse got so desperate at all of this talk that he took action. While no one was watching, Mouse crept in through a back entrance of the cave, that only a mouse could know, and gnawed the bowstrings of the two sisters' bows three-quarters of the way through, so that they looked strong and gave no evidence of having been tampered with, but would break the moment any tension was put on them. He came back and announced what he had done, and Wolf took credit for it, but Coyote said, no, it was his idea, and there was more interminable talk between them. Well, what to do about the antelope? Wolf had great, long plans for this, and Coyote had even longer plans for this, and the two of them got to arguing for weeks and weeks, and everybody was growing desperate all at this talk, which was burdening their ears so terribly.

Rattlesnake couldn't stand it anymore and wriggled off through the rocks. He was so well-camouflaged and was so much a part of the sand that he got close to the antelope with an eye at the end of every hair without being seen, and when the moment was right, he struck out and killed the antelope. He came back and told everyone what had happened, and Wolf took all the credit for this, but Coyote said, no, it was his mastermind plan, and there was more quarreling. Wolf had many ideas on how to attack Old Stoneshirt, and Coyote had even more ideas, and more weeks went by until everybody was just at the edge of their sanity.

Rattlesnake couldn't stand it any longer, and once again, he went off and observed the daily habits of Old Stoneshirt. He noticed that Old Stoneshirt had at least one human characteristic left in him, and that was that he went down to a particular spot in the meadow to answer the call of nature every morning. Rattlesnake observed this very carefully, and one morning he hid himself at just the right spot. Then at the critical moment, he struck. He bit Old Stoneshirt in the one vulnerable place which he had been unable to cover with stone, and he killed him. He came back and announced that Old Stoneshirt was dead, and Wolf immediately took credit for all of this, but Coyote said, no, it was his master plan which had accomplished all of this, and they talked absolutely interminably, but no one minded very much because they were all so happy at what had happened.

While the two were talking, and celebrations were being made, One-Two Man went to the cave and found his mother. He brought her out, and the two of them went away happily together.

Chapter 4
Savatri and Satchavan
Introduced by Laurie Downs
and Elizabeth Rucker

We met Robert Johnson in 1983 at our first Journey Into Wholeness Conference in St. Simons Island, Georgia. Our introduction was brief but unforgettable. We were in a "staff meeting" and all seated in a circle. Robert appeared, and it was clearly understood by everyone that he was the "sage" of the group. He spoke softly, but with perfect diction, undeniable intelligence, and grace. It was difficult not to feel reverence when he spoke. We were there to present art therapy workshops and share our "story" of love and healing.

We became members of the large Journey Into Wholeness family and attended every year from that time until the end of its days in 2007. Every year, we looked forward to being there for this "family reunion" and being in the presence of such remarkable people. Our staff meetings continued. Many were like us—workshop presenters and helpers. Others were lecturers and the leaders, Annette and Jim Cullipher. That side of the group was the mysterious ones, the ones who spoke deeply of the unconscious and told stories of how we could heal our inner beings. Robert was in this group, but he always stood apart as the Master of some realm, the imaginal realms, that we were not seeing. We looked forward to seeing him every year in his dark pants, crisp white shirt, and tie. He walked with a limp, and it was not until years later that we realized he had an artificial leg. This only added to his mystery. His lectures were bursting with knowledge and countless layers of wisdom.

One of our favorite memories of Robert was his love of precious and semi-precious stones and gems. He carried some in his pockets and often shared them with people. Sometimes in those staff meetings he would lay them out and allow us to choose our gem. We all learned soon enough that Robert was there to share many "gems," especially as the storykeeper and storyteller. Every evening after the final lecture, he would share a story. Sometimes they were stories of whimsy, sometimes they were full of fear and death, and sometimes they were laden with meaning that took days to unpack. But there was always a theme and always substance and significance.

As with the story of Savatri and Satchavan, all of the stories were lined with deep meaning, imagery, and heartfelt sentiments. This story resonated clearly with us. We were led to Journey in the midst of our own great passage into pure love. We would do anything to be with each other and knew that, in some mysterious way, it was forever. One of us, Laurie, was attempting to live through a life-threatening illness and the other, Elizabeth, was moving toward divorce. Both of us were, at this time and continuing to this day, using art as a tool for healing and better understanding. Both of us were deeply in love and needed the support of this family to survive and live out our destinies. Over the many years with Robert and Journey Into Wholeness, we were in the maelstrom of living through great hardships. It was as if the God of Death, Yama, had already begun to pluck out our souls and take us both. Many Journey conferences were spent with one of us being ill and one of us in excruciating grief. Long into our time as a couple, we were blessed with better health and healing. Now, many years later, we know we cheated death in some way through the immeasurable miracles of love between us and within this community and others. The story of Savatri and Savatchan is indeed the story of cheating death and living into the dream of life and life beyond death. They lived into the life they wanted, filled with love, creativity, and abundance in the center of community. This is where we find ourselves, full, grateful, and living a dream.

Elizabeth Rucker is an artist and retired Art Therapist. Laurie Downs is a retired registered nurse and artist. They live peacefully on a mountain in Asheville, North Carolina, surrounded by their beautiful gardens, nature at its best, and loving animals.

Once long, long, ago, there was a king. He was the king of Madras, a province of India far south on the east coast. He and his wife ruled a beautiful kingdom, a happy kingdom, and everything was well. He was known as the great king, but there was one great unhappiness in the life of the king and the queen of Madras, and that was they had no children. This weighed heavily on their hearts and their minds, and years went by with no heirs. Finally, the time for children was drawing to a close, so the king declared a month of puja, a month of time for worship, for supplication, for prayer, for asceticism, to beg the gods, finally, for a child.

The puja was so great and so deep that not even the gods could ignore it, and the queen conceived a child. They were overjoyed, and they might have worried that the child wouldn't come to term as the queen was some time past her youth, but somehow it never occurred to them to worry about it, and they were right. The child was born in due time. There was a slight moment of disappointment because it was a girl, not a boy, and they had hoped for an heir to the throne as was important for a king. But they were delighted with the girl, and they named her Savatri, which means "that which contains all virtue." The girl lived up to her name and she was a happy child. She was bright, she was clear, she was intelligent, and she was a courteous soul from the very beginning. She delighted her parents and she delighted the kingdom.

Savatri grew, and the kingdom revolved around this happy, bright, cheerful, lively child. It was a custom of India that one of the profound duties of a father was to find a suitable husband for his daughter by her sixteenth birthday, the marriage date for Indians. The king didn't want to lose her, and he knew very well that her husband, who of course must be of royal lineage himself, would take her off to his own kingdom, as was proper. The king dreaded this, but he was brave, and he put the happiness of his daughter and the adherence of custom before his own wishes.

Savatri came to be sixteen, and the king inquired of the neighboring kingdoms whether there was an eligible son who might take a wife and grace that kingdom with a queen of the quality of Savatri. But one thing or another got in the way, and the young men were engaged otherwise. Sixteen came and went, and the king began to worry that he was derelict in his duty.

Finally, he did an unheard-of thing, and he asked Savatri, "Well, who would you like to marry?"

This was unheard of, and at least a thousand years ahead of its time, and Savatri said, "I don't know anybody who I wish to marry. I'm happy as I am."

So sixteen came and went, and heaven forbid, seventeen came and went, and still no husband for Savatri.

Now it was custom in the olden times that there was always a group of holy men, highly revered in their kingdom, who would live across the river within a few hours' walk of the palace, and they lived on the hill known as the holy hill. Savatri went every day to study with the greatest and best of all the holy men who lived at the top of holy hill. She went there with great joy, and sat at the feet of the holy man and took part in his teachings with a dozen or so other students, both young men and young women, as it was an enlightened and intelligent kingdom. The group was delighted with Savatri, because she was the brightest, clearest, and cleverest of all the students. The holy man, though observing his detachment in life, was secretly terribly pleased with Savatri. Savatri was very pleased with her studies, and you could hardly imagine a more tranquil scene than Savatri leaving the royal palace in the morning, and, with her brightness and her cheerfulness, going across the river with the ferrymen, and going up the hill to sit with the dozen other students at the feet of the great holy man.

One day she was going up the hill in the bright sunshine of the morning, and her eyes fell upon the most handsome young man she had ever seen in her life. In an instant, as is the case of things that are divinely inspired, she gave her heart to that man without question, without rumination, and without reservation. And when an Indian maid gave her heart to a man, it happened only once within her lifetime, and should that man die she would never marry again, nor would she look at another man with the eyes of courtship. Whether it was in accordance with divine law, or whether it was some of the unfairness of the patriarchal world, if a man lost his wife, he may marry again, but not so with a woman. Savatri knew this in a flash of a second, and she knew the only man who was to be of any importance in her life stood before her. She lowered her eyes demurely, and went on to her lesson.

She was curiously silent in her lesson that morning. The holy man, who knew all, knew what had happened. He read it in Savatri's eyes, or in his interior eyes he knew, and he had a small smile on his face as he taught, for he knew that a great moment had come for his beloved Savatri. Savatri tarried after her lessons, and discreetly asked about the newcomer.

The holy man said, "Oh, he is indeed a prince, though you would never know it because he lives in abject poverty. His father, who was the king of the neighboring kingdom, ruled his kingdom with such mildness and generosity that the evil ones of the kingdom took the power away from him, blinded him, and sent him off into exile. So, the blinded king and his son, Satchavan, have arrived only yesterday to live on holy hill, and to pass the rest of the days of the king's life in this manner."

Savatri was secretly delighted to find that the young man that she had fallen in love with was truly a prince, both outwardly and inwardly.

She went back to the palace, and, being the bright and spritely soul that she was, went to her father and said, "Father, I have found my husband, and his name is Satchavan, and he lives on holy hill, and he is the son of a king."

The father was delighted because his duty was accomplished, but he was sad because the time was approaching when his daughter would leave him. He agreed to Savatri's request. He went over to holy hill afterward, sought out the blind king, and asked for permission that the son should marry Savatri. The blind king delighted at this, Savatri delighted, and Satchavan was not consulted.

The next thing to do was to go to the holy man and consult him as to the future of all of this.

The king went to the holy man, explained everything unnecessarily to him, and said, "What do you think of the marriage?"

The holy man said, "There is none wiser or deeper or better than Satchavan, and Savatri could not marry a better man, but I advise against it."

The king was greatly distraught at this, because darkness and despair was in the air.

The king said, "Why not?" The holy man did not answer, but only looked down.

The king said, "Why? Is he not wise?"

The holy man said, "He is wise like the eagle."

"Does he not have fidelity?"

"He has fidelity like the antelope."

"Is he not strong?"

"He is strong like the lion."

"Can he not bear children?"

"He can bear children like the bull."

"Is he not persevering?"

"He is persevering like the hawk."

And on through many, many, many virtues, and finally the king burst forth, "Then why? Why do you advise against a marriage to Satchavan?"

The holy man, caught in one of the rare times of his life when he was embarrassed at his intentions, was drawing circles in the dust with his toe.

He said, "Because it is the fate that Satchavan will die one year from today, and your daughter will be a widow within the year."

Terrible sadness fell over both of them, and the king went home, summoned Savatri, and said, "The signs are that you should not marry Satchavan."

Savatri demanded to know why, and finally the king told her.

Savatri knew immediately what to do. "I would rather have one year of marriage with my beloved than to lose him and not know him at all."

The king conceded to this, and since time was going very rapidly, he arranged that many of the ceremonies of the wedding should be curtailed, and Savatri and Satchavan were soon married.

Savatri, the princess of the kingdom of Madras, was taken home to a mud hut on holy hill and tended to her husband Satchavan with much tenderness and never complained for lack of servants, or the downcoming of her life. The year went by remarkably fast. Somebody once said that happiness has no history, and there was no history for those two. Savatri woke up one day to the fact that the year was very close to expiring, and she got into a total panic. She was fluttering around Satchavan, watching over him, trying to protect him, covering him with all the love she could muster. Finally, the awful, awful day came. Savatri had been fasting for three days in preparation, clutching at any straw she could to save her beloved.

The dreaded day came and Satchavan, who had not been told about any of this, said, "We need wood. I will go out and I will cut wood today."

Savatri's heart failed her at that moment, the sight of Satchavan with an axe in his hand too much for her.

She tried to prevail upon him not to go, but he said, "Of course I will go."

So she said, "May I come with you?"

"No, no, it's a hot day, and woodcutting is dull. You stay, and I will be back at sunset."

But Savatri insisted on going. She watched, and every glint of the sun on the blade of the axe was a horror to her, and she watched just like a hawk. Noon came, and Satchavan sat himself down to eat lunch and sleep for the two or three hottest hours of the day and resume his work later in the afternoon. Savatri was fluttering about him, performing every ministration she could for him. She poured him water, she combed his hair, she bathed his face. Satchavan was very pleased with this, but was confused by it, as he didn't know what an awful day it was.

Finally, he went to sleep, and a few minutes later Savatri was horrified, absolutely struck cold with terror, to see a stranger approaching. And she half knew but half refused to know who the stranger was. The stranger was no less than Yama, the God of Death, whose job it was to come and extract the soul of the dead, wrap it in a cord, tuck the cord into the pocket of his garment, and take it into the next world.

Savatri, clutching the last possible straw, threw herself at the feet of Yama and said, "Oh great stranger, you dressed in a black coat with red lining, I beg of you to save the soul of my beloved!" and she poured out the story. Even Yama, the God of Death, was touched by the story, but he was bound by duty.

He said, "I am the god Yama, and I have come for the soul of your beloved, and it cannot be otherwise."

Savatri, in the face of the God of Death, grew quiet. She backed off two paces and watched while Yama deftly plucked the soul out of Satchavan. As everyone knows, the soul lives in the secret most cavern in the center of the heart, and is the size of a thumb. Yama extracted the soul, bound it with his cord, tucked it into his pouch, and turned reluctantly, never having had a harder job with a mortal human, and began to walk away. He had walked some distance when he heard the sound of someone accompanying him. Soon he was to reach that boundary between this world and the next world, where everything grew dim and began to lose its corporeal nature, and turned into that of the next world.

So Yama, growing a little transparent and a little thin, turned around and he said, "Maid, turn and go back, I implore you. We are approaching the boundary of the next world, and no mortal may come."

Savatri said, "I will come with you."

Yama winced, and he said, "No, you may not come with me, as mortals may not come into the next world. It will be time enough soon when I will come to get your soul and pluck it out and bind it and take it to the next world, but it is not time yet. You must still live out your allotted years."

He turned to walk on, but he heard the crackling of feet in the brush and he turned around. Savatri was still there, both of them growing thinner and more transparent as they neared the other world.

Yama said, "Maid, please, I beg you, turn around. I will give you any wish you ask, except the life of your husband, if you will turn around and go back."

Savatri said, "Please, return the sight of Satchavan's father."

Yama said, "It is so, the instant you asked it, it is so. Now please leave."

He went on a little farther, but still there was the sound of walking behind him, so he turned and said, "Maid, please go back, ask anything you wish, except the life of your husband, and you may have it, but you must go back."

Savatri said, "My father shall have sons and heirs."

Yama, the God of Death, said, "It is so, simply as you ask it, it is so. Now, you must go back."

And he walked on, in turmoil. But he heard the sounds of feet behind him and turned around and said, "For the last time, before I have to bring my thunderbolt, which I have by virtue of being the God of Death, ask anything but the life of your husband and I will give it to you."

And she said, "I will have many sons."

Yama, the God of Death, desperate at this time, said, "It is so, it shall be so, now turn around and go back."

Savatri jumped with joy. "Now, I have you! Because an Indian maid may have her sons only by her husband, it would be illegal, it would be immoral, it would be unthinkable for me to have sons by anyone but my one and only love in the world. Now you must give me back Satchavan, so that we may have many sons."

Yama groaned that he had been tricked, and he said, "Alright, alright, alright."

He turned his footsteps back to the not yet cooled corpse of Satchavan, sleeping beside his axe. He took the soul, which is the size of a thumb, unbound it from its cord, tucked it neatly back into that cavern in the secret most place of the heart, and both were delighted to see life return to the body of Satchavan. He sat up, stretched, and said, "I've had the strangest dream! I can't describe it." Savatri did not ask.

Satchavan cut wood for the rest of the afternoon. Savatri prayed every prayer of thanksgiving which she knew, and they went back home again. The King and Queen of Madras had sons and heirs. The father of Satchavan miraculously recovered his sight and he went back with the aid of the King of Madras to regain his kingdom. Satchavan returned to his native kingdom, became king soon after, and Savatri was queen of the realm. They did, indeed, have many sons and many years of happiness.

Chapter 5
Cry of the Loon
Introduced by Barry Williams

Robert and I tried a number of ways to converse for a few years, but failed to find an adequate platform for sustained communication until we discovered we could speak dreams to each other. We shared a deeply introverted feeling function, he much more than I, that would not easily allow the enormity of the meaning and value of what we knew to rise to the level of vocabulary and expression. But when we spoke dreams, the meaning laden images that became words between us carried the weight of that place and understanding that could not otherwise be expressed. To relate to him in that way was like riding on the back of the loon in this Inuit story.

I knew Robert best from his years at the Temagami Vision Quest, and when he would step out of the float plane onto the dock, he would invariably greet me with, "I have a dream for you."

And I would respond that I had a dream for him.

There was no small talk with Robert, which was why he loved his time in the North with us, because it was intense, real, and essential time and communication in the heart of nature.

One day, sitting together in silence, he said out of the blue, "Anything with an opposite is not worth having."

Or another time, he said that Nature would act on the human world in the same way that the collective unconscious could act on the ego when it is dangerously out of alignment, sweeping away the ego's old position, so life could order itself around a new center. The story of the boy and the loon certainly contains that dynamic, and we may be seeing that time now in the world.

Robert loved stories that would leave his listeners puzzled by the inability of the mind to grasp the deeper meaning, pushing them toward symbolic thought. He would tell this pan-Arctic myth in preparation for the vision quest as an image of turning toward nature to ask for help with an otherwise unsolvable problem of one's blindness. The negative mother complex inhibits life through a regressive pull toward the unconscious, creating an impoverishment of the soul. Climbing on the back of the loon, whose call is heard day and night in the North, is to be taken deeper, over and over, to the ego's felt limits, to restore the kind of sight that only comes from the darkness of the impossible depths. This consciousness sees the greater world beyond the ruling complex and liberates one to live more freely.

The boy's negative mother complex nearly fatally weakens his otherwise strong masculinity through a blinding of lies, humiliation, and deflation. When he finally sees the truth, he takes decisive, potent action against the complex. He hears and heeds the call of the loon that he intuitively knows is his inner healer, the guide to his own depths, from which his true life will come. Robert loved this part of all stories, where the mysterious and autonomous guidance of the unconscious takes over. The loon is the medicine of depth, inwardness, and the redemptive struggle for sight in the darkness. It is the story of the vision quest and the transformational contact with the archetypal world.

"The psyche is fascinated by transformation," he said to me once in talking about the value of stories.

The lysis of the story is about living with the enormous energy released through a healing of the central complex. The old structures of identity, family, and culture can no longer contain who you have become in your individuation journey. Overcoming the disabling effects of his complex gives the boy new life, vision, and potency. He outgrows his old life and has to leave to seek a new one. As Robert well knew, this can happen in any life when the archetypal world reveals itself in dramatic fashion in an analysis, dream, vision quest, or life event. In celebrating his new-found life, the boy unwittingly becomes incestuously too close to his own soul, his inner being as the sister anima, in an unintentional but fated encounter with over-whelming energies, forcing him into a cosmic, archetypal reality imagined as the sun and moon. The story is a warning, guide, and description about the great forces in life that can heal and transform, and the taboos that push one too far into an archetypal identification, which few survive. Great shamans are made of such fateful, initiatory events. What begins in utter unconscious, complex misery, ends in the highest attainment.

Robert wanted people, through this story, to consider their own complexes, healing, potentials, self-imposed restrictions, initiatory experiences, and individuation journeys. He would be pleased to hear us discussing it and wrestling with it.

Barry Williams M.Div., Psy.D., is a Jungian analyst living near Taos, New Mexico, and is a mara'akame in the Huichol tradition.

Long before the beginning of time, there was a little Native American family, way, way up north in Canada. It was a pitiful family, because the father was dead, and the only son was blind. There was a law in Native American families that only a man could hunt or shoot, so this family eked out a very precarious existence. The mother took the boy out hunting, and when the mother saw game, she directed the boy where to shoot. Once in a while, the arrow met its prey and the family had a little bit to eat, but not very often. It was a very thin living, indeed, that they had.

One day they were out, and the mother saw a bear and whispered to the boy, "Over there, just a bit farther, a bit more to the right, down a little, now shoot!"

The boy shot, and the arrow hit the heart of the bear. The bear fell over, and then the most dreadful thing happened.

The mother said, "Oh, you missed."

They went home, and the mother quietly went back and got the bear, carried it in, and said, "See what I got!"

The boy felt terrible, and the sister who knew all about this said nothing. They feasted on bear for several fine and filling days, but the boy was miserable because he thought he had missed. The sister could stand it no longer, and she took her blind brother off and told him what had happened. The boy got into a rage, and he came at his mother and he killed her.

Then they were in a worse situation than before, because it was just the blind boy and his younger sister. Because killing one's mother was such a terrible taboo, they had to leave their tribe. So off they went, and they lived an even more miserable existence. They got some berries, and occasionally the sister would see game and direct the boy on where to shoot, but they just barely managed.

One day they were walking along in the forest. As you know, if one faculty is missing in a person, some other faculty can grow very acute. This is what happened with this boy. His eyesight was gone, so his sense of hearing had grown very keen. They were walking near a lake, and the boy heard the cry of a loon, and discovered that the loon was calling his name. By following the direction of the cries, the boy came to the edge of a lake.

The loon came and guided the boy into the lake. Loons are famous for their ability to dive and can go two or three hundred feet below the water. The loon took the boy down in a short dive and brought him back up. This loon called every day, and the boy heard the cry and came. Each day they dived, and each day the loon went a little bit deeper. With every dive, a little bit of eyesight returned to the boy. Finally, when the loon could take the boy on the deepest dive and the boy could hold his breath and survive, the boy's eyesight was completely restored.

It was a wonderful time and a cause for great celebration. The brother and sister laughed and were happy, a feeling they had seldom felt. The boy was now able to hunt, but they still couldn't return to their tribe.

Eventually, they came to a village that was celebrating a festival day. Everybody was preparing and there was to be a great dance that night where they would all be in beautiful costumes. The village welcomed the boy and girl, and helped them to find attire so they could participate. The boy and his sister had never experienced this sort of welcome and they were overjoyed.

That evening they danced, and they danced, and they danced, and the more they danced the happier they were.

The boy and girl thought, "Wonderful, we have a community again, we belong."

They danced all night. The culmination of the dance was that at the crack of dawn, when the medicine man clapped his hands, you would go home with whatever partner you had in your arms and you would make love. Everybody was happy with this, and at the crack of dawn the medicine man clapped his hands and they all went back to their houses and made love.

The boy woke up in the morning and took off his costume. His partner also took off her costume and, in horror, he realized he had spent the night with his sister. This was almost the only other taboo that would end in excommunication. The tribe discovered what had happened and threw them out of the community. This was the law, an absolute, and there were no exceptions.

The boy and the girl were homeless and alone again. They had no place to go and were very discouraged and very lonely. They had each other, but they didn't have a community. Finally, they grew so lonely, and the energy had drained out of them so badly, that the great spirit took pity on them and lifted them into the sky. This was how the sun and the moon came into existence. The great aloneness of the sky was the only place that a pair like this, who had broken such severe taboos, could live.

Chapter 6
The Frog Queen
Introduced by Rob Luke

My relationship with Robert Johnson is most likely quite different than that of most of you reading these stories and myths. I have never attended one of his workshops and I have never been a student of psychology.

I remember clearly meeting Robert for the first time as he stood with my mother, Helen Luke, waiting for our rag-tag and bobtailed group to arrive in Los Angeles from England. Nick, my brother, Mrs. Mitchell, our housekeeper, Betty, her daughter, and me. I remember holding out my hand to take his.

There was this VERY tall, slender man leaning in to greet me, asking, "What is your name?"

Of course, he knew my name full well, but I replied, "Robert."

He promptly stated, "Well, that is a very fine name—it's my name too. There cannot be two Roberts in one home. How will we know which one they are calling for when supper is ready? Therefore, you will be known as Rob, and I shall be known as Bob."

Thus began my lifelong relationship with Robert "Bob" Johnson. He was my guide, my tutor, my advisor, and my beloved father figure from the age of six.

The correlation that I draw between the Frog Queen story, Robert, and myself is hidden until almost the end of the story. Many may not be aware that Robert Johnson was an extremely talented musician. During the first part of his life, music was extremely important and entirely filled his world. He was a talented organist and harpsichordist. He continued to play for pleasure in later years and enjoyed his beautiful harpsichords and clavichords, but writing, lecturing, and helping others became the main focus of his life.

Through Robert's guidance, I had a wonderful up-bringing and was encouraged to diligently follow my path. I was good with numbers and when selecting a college path, I thought of engineering. However, Robert's beautiful music had filled my world, affected my deeper thoughts, and influenced my hidden dreams. I was a young adult striving to be practical and follow a path to future employment, but music totally overwhelmed me. Maybe Robert felt slightly guilty for surrounding me with music, but he still encouraged me to follow my dream. He bought me a beautiful Viola da Gamba and together we played many concerts together. He encouraged me and guided me. Due entirely to Robert, I went on to follow my heart, study in Europe, and became a cellist.

So, like the king in the story, we both faced our own reality and found the courage to embrace our true passion. We both killed many frogs on our journey before facing that which we could not escape. He, to give up full-time music to face the outer world he had so tried to avoid. To face the reality of helping others through his writing and lecturing. And me, with his guidance and encouragement, to become a musician and find my passion through music.

Robert Luke became a professional cellist and a university professor because of Robert's musical talent, passion, and influence, and his family found a new home in America with Robert. In later life, he has been an appraiser of fine arts and antiques.

There was once a young king, a fine king. He was loved by his subjects and was vigorous and strong. He was a fine man in every respect, and he loved to hunt. One day, he was out with his courtiers, galloping along and hunting. The king saw a deer and he veered off and began to follow it. This miraculous deer always kept just outside of the range of bow and arrow. The king was half-maddened by this, and he plunged further and further into the forest after the deer, and got himself totally lost. He didn't even notice he was lost because he was so intent upon getting this prized deer. He chased the deer all day, and finally, when he was irretrievably lost in the forest, the deer simply vanished.

The king was now exhausted, bewildered, a little frightened as he was separated from all of his courtiers, and very far into the forest. Being a wise man, he got off his horse and sat still. When you don't know the best thing to do, the wise thing is to just keep still. While he was sitting in the late afternoon calm and beauty, he heard the most beautiful singing. It was a song he had never heard before and he knew by the sound of her voice that the maiden singing this song was quite fair. He fell in love with the voice. He got up, and he began moving in the direction of the sound on foot, and soon came upon the maiden. She was, indeed, as lovely as her voice had been, and the king lost his heart to her instantly. He was completely overwhelmed by the beauty of the maiden.

He said to the maiden, "Are you married? Are you given in marriage? Are you betrothed? Has your father promised you?"

And the maiden said, "No, none of those."

"So you shall be my queen."

"Well, you must ask my father. That is not for me to say."

So, the king said, "Take me to your father," and she did.

The old father, a pretty wise man, was delighted to have a king as a son-in-law, but he didn't let his enthusiasm get too obvious.

The father said, "Yes, you may have my daughter as your queen, but on one condition: she must never see water."

This didn't seem like a very big deal for the king, if that was all that was required. He agreed immediately. So, they were married and it was a great wedding worthy of the king. Everyone was very happy. The king took his queen back to his kingdom and was well received, but then there was the small business of keeping the queen from ever seeing water. This is Indian mythology, and is to be interpreted just slightly differently from our own; if you would replace the word "water" in the rest of the story with the word "reality," it would be better understood.

The king arranged that the queen should see no water. It was difficult from the very beginning, because the royal palace was built on the river that ran through the royal city. So, immediately, the king had to have the river-facing side of the palace bricked up. The king spent an inordinate amount of time arranging that the queen should never see water. He would take her up on the roof garden occasionally, but he had to be very careful that there was no rainstorm in sight. Before long, the king was spending all his time protecting the queen from seeing any water, and was doing nothing else. He was ignoring his kingly duties and the kingdom was going to seed very badly.

Finally, the courtiers came to him and said, "We can't have an audience with you and you are not managing the kingdom. We are lodging a complaint."

The king said, "I have no time. Go away, I'm busy."

Finally, the head courtier saw that the kingdom was in dire danger, and there was no use asking the king as he was out of his head these days. So, the head courtier went to the servants and asked how the palace worked, and what they did for the king.

The servants said, "We spend our entire time making sure the queen does not see any water."

The head courtier came to the king and said, "I have learned of your difficulty. Let's work something out. We will improve the garden on the rooftop of the palace. A roof will be put over it, so if it rains you will have no difficulty. You and the queen can be happy again."

So they did this, and it was fine.

But the courtier said to the king, "Are you not thirsty and hungry for the sight of water?"

The king said, "I am famished for water, but I don't dare look or the queen might be in trouble."

The courtier said, "Alright, we will put a fountain in the middle of the garden. We will surround it so thoroughly that the queen need never see it, and you may go in private to the fountain and be refreshed."

This was done, and the king went daily to the fountain and was pleased with it. But one day, inevitably, the queen went in and found the fountain and was delighted with it. Of course, upon gazing at it, she instantly vanished. The king was absolutely overcome with loneliness. Everything that he had wanted in the world, that he'd had a touch of, was gone. He was inconsolable and he could not eat and he could not drink. There was nothing to assuage his loneliness. The courtiers all tried to cheer him, they gave him the best of everything, but someone who is attacked by that kind of loneliness is inconsolable, and there's nothing anybody can do for such a person. There is no amount of money, fame, possessions, entertainment, or anything else that can break through that incurable kind of loneliness. The king now lived in the bottom level of hell, which was frozen over.

A wise man in the palace had observed that the moment the queen vanished, a small, insignificant frog appeared next to the fountain. This wise man was very observant. He didn't know what this meant, but he observed.

The king, when he could function again, heard about the frog at the fountain. With his own hands he went up and he smashed it flat. In such a fury, he sent word out around the kingdom that all the frogs were to be killed. A ludicrous sight ensued. For weeks, peasants were seen trudging toward the palace with sacks of dead frogs on their backs to collect the bounty. Finally, so many frogs had been killed that few were left in the whole of the kingdom. The frog king came to the king, and since they were both kings of their realms, they respected each other.

The frog king said, "You are about to exterminate the race of frogs, and I have to tell you that I am the father of your queen. She has returned to the land of frogs because you broke your vow."

The king heard, he listened, and he made peace with the frog king. The frog king brought his daughter, the little frog, back to her womanly form. It was the queen in all of her glory, and all of her beauty. The king embraced her, happy again, and from that moment on the queen was no longer required to stay away from water.

Chapter 7
The Dame Ragnel
Introduced by Paula Reeves

Robert Johnson was a masterful storyteller. He knew the potency of a metaphor, which, when received by the listener, can simultaneously interest the intellect, energize the body, and evoke the soul. Robert's investment in story is rooted in the humus of what Jung described as the collective unconscious: the richly layered, symbolic language of thousands of years of humans trying to understand how to be fully human in a soul-filled body.

To answer this question, Robert dipped into his beloved myth, The Grail Quest, and summoned the conundrum of The Dame Ragnel. As a Mythographer, someone who uses myth to describe the development of the body, the individuation of the psyche, and the symbolic nature of dreams, I value Dame Ragnel's story as one of the few that leads us straight to the body.

"What," the story asks, "does a woman want?"

"Sovereignty," is the reply. Ownership over her own matter—mater—mother.

One year, Robert and I taught the Grail Myth in tandem. He from the perspective of the masculine, and I from the feminine. I mentioned to Robert that he had met the Dame Ragnel at a young age when he lost a portion of his leg in an accident. He sat silently, pondering, and later said it was so. His body, in her recovery, asked for sensitivity and compassion. He had never thought of his own dear leg that way before. Individuation invites courage, surrender—without collapse—and an open heart.

Robert was a man who lived his life led by his inner work. If he believed in something, he was highly disciplined. Prior to his giving a lecture, I would frequently hear him in the room adjacent to mine rehearsing the telling of a myth. He would do this several times without changing a word. His inner work and his outer work were done with great discipline and intention. He said he had only one life to live and to live otherwise, for him, would be folly.

Knowing Robert, teaching together, and sharing innumerable conversations for over two decades left me with life lessons that continue to sustain me into my eighth decade as I prepare for the ending of my own life. He did this for so many.

Gawain said, "You choose, My Lady."

We're told that at that moment all the bells in the land pealed. Bless you, dear Robert, for teaching us to be more fully human.

Paula Reeves is a body-oriented Jungian psycho-therapist. She has written two books, *Woman's Intuition: Unlocking the Wisdom of the Body*, and *Heart Sense: Unlocking Your Highest Purpose and Deepest Desires*. She is the creator of *Mindful Mirroring* and *Spontaneous Contemplative Movement*. She is in private practice in Atlanta, Georgia.

It might come as a shock to find that King Arthur, as a youth in his teens, was caught poaching salmon in the stream of a neighboring kingdom. He climbed up into a tree when he saw the king of the adjoining realm coming, and tried to avoid being caught, but he could not.

The neighboring king, a kind man essentially, said, "You know, the law is that I should kill you right now, caught in the act. I don't have to take you to the court. I don't have to take you home. The law says I should kill you, but I'll be more merciful than that. I will ask you a question, and if you can bring the answer to this question back one year from today, you'll be free. Otherwise, off with your head."

Arthur agreed to seek the answer, clearly the better of the options, and went home. He was pretty happy for a day or two, but after asking around among his friends, he realized that finding the answer to this baffling question would not be as easy as he had thought. He had begun to learn the magnitude of his task. The question was, "What does a woman really want?" He asked everybody he could ask, but he only got answers he knew were inadequate. He spent the whole year seeking, and worrying more and more.

Finally, somebody said, "There's only one person in the kingdom who can answer that question for you, and that's the old hideous damsel, Dame Ragnel. She's a beast, and she charges an arm and a leg for her wisdom, but she'll know."

So, Arthur went about asking anybody else he could think of, and on the last day he finally went to Dame Ragnel. The Dame Ragnel was a God-awful creature. She had a humpback, she drizzled, her hair was a mess, she smelled, and her manners were nonexistent. But she had power.

Dame Ragnel said, "Yes, I'll give you an answer to your question, but you must understand, my fee is high."

Arthur was afraid, but the alternative was his neck.

He said, "I agree to your fee," and the old woman gave him the answer.

He took the answer to the neighboring kingdom on the appointed day, and told the king what he had learned. The king was impressed and knew the answer was correct.

"What does a woman really want? She wants sovereignty over her own life."

Now, what was the fee, you ask? The fee was that the old hideous damsel would be given in marriage to Arthur's best friend, Gawain. Arthur was mortified by this. He wasn't going to feed his best friend to this horrible dragon of a woman, and he thought he'd rather get his own head cut off than go through with this. He got himself into a terrible state, moped around, wouldn't eat anything, and wouldn't speak.

Finally, Gawain, being a blood-brother and so close to Arthur, couldn't bear it.

"What's the matter? I'm your best friend and brother. Please tell me what ails you. What dreadful thing has come?"

Arthur wouldn't tell him. Gawain went away, and he sought out information everywhere until he found out what was bothering his good friend.

He went to Arthur and said, "For my friend and for my king, I will do this for you. I will marry the hideous damsel."

Arthur was still reluctant, but neck versus friend, and friend being compliant, he agreed.

So, the wedding was set up, and it was the greatest of all the weddings in the kingdom. Everyone from everywhere was invited. At the banquet table, Gawain sat at one end and the ghastly Dame sat at the other, making the most disgusting noises and smells. She was hideous beyond any description. She was rude, she snuffled, and she ate straight off of her plate like an animal. She was at her very worst for these royal people. But Gawain sat there nobly, and was courteous to her.

Then, they were off to the wedding chamber, where even worse awaited. Gawain stripped himself down and got into bed to wait for his hideous wife. She was off dressing in the alcove, and when she came back (having left sufficient time for Gawain to worry himself into a state), she was a ravishingly beautiful maiden.

She said to Gawain, "Alright, you have been courteous to me, you have respected me, and you have given me honor. Because of this, I will be hideous damsel to you half the time, and fair maiden to you half the time. Which will it be? Hideous damsel embarrassing you in your world by day and lovely maiden in your bed, or beautiful and charming maiden on your arm during the day and hideous witch in your bed?"

Gawain thought for a while, and said, "I will let you choose."

The Dame Ragnel said, "For this added honor and respect, I will be fair maiden for you day and night."

Chapter 8
The King and the Sannyasin
Introduced by Pete Williams

It was my first experience with Journey Into Wholeness. I had just turned 44. I knew no one there. I knew nothing of Carl Jung. My outer life was in chaos—marriage, career, purpose, and I was there only because my wise therapist told me I should be there. There was much talk of this guy Robert Johnson, "a wise man," people said. With no expectation or understanding, I went to his workshop on dreams. Robert spoke to our small group and told us of a recent dream in which he was at a seaside setting, walking along a beach. He described that all in the dream was gray—the beach, the sky, the sea, the landscape. And that was it. That was the dream. I was left feeling most unsettled, but with no understanding of why.

Later that day, as I entered the dining room, I found myself face to face with Robert. He was leaving and I was going in.

From a place somewhere within me I think I now know something about, I said, "Robert, hearing you tell of your dream has so upset me. I thought you were someone who had figured this all out."

He put his hand on my shoulder and simply said, "We need to talk." And then he walked away.

A few days later, we found that time "to talk." A relationship began that week, and for many years after that Robert was for me many things: the positive father, the caring grandfather, a mentor, and a guide—"the wise man."

Robert understood that it is through myth, fairy tale, and story that humankind expresses and records those collective, archetypal dreams that bring meaning to the human experience. He favored story. As in a dream, these stories give image and voice to aspects of our personalities that are out of balance. They have perhaps fallen out of connection and been split off from consciousness, or they are parts of ourselves in conflict or tension that have fallen into shadow. Perhaps they are aspects of ourselves that are simply, as yet, unknown.

Like a dream, "The King and the Sannyasin" can be understood on many levels and interpreted in many ways. One musing I had was to reflect on the story as a tale of the ongoing individuation process. The "holy man" seems to hold the center throughout the story, and he is an image of the "spiritus rector" which Jung often mentions in his writings. The king is ruling the outer world in an excellent fashion, while also focusing on the teachings of the holy man who holds knowledge of the inner world. The Sannyasin seems to wander between these worlds. I wonder, is the king a shadow figure for the Sannyasin, or is the Sannyasin a shadow for the king?

Then, a fire breaks out. An imbalance occurs. We all know this in our lives, disruptions that challenge us at our core. It's occurring in the world around me as I write this. As an individuation story, it is in these moments that we are given the choice to grow or regress, to enlarge or diminish. In the story, balance returns—the fire is out, and the palace is restored. And that restoration occurs when the Sannyasin comes to some new level of awareness, when he is called to consciousness by the holy man. But the story does not tell us what the Sannyasin does with his new awareness. We don't know how he understands the question, "Now, who is more attached to his property?"

I'm writing this introduction at home in the midst of the palace fire of the COVID-19 pandemic. All of us are now being called to a new awareness of what we value. And what will we do?

Pete Williams, Ph.D., LPC, is a Jungian Psychoanalyst in private practice in Atlanta, Georgia. He trained with the Inter-Regional Society of Jungian Analysts and is currently serving as the Director of Training.

Once, long ago, there was a very fine king. He ruled an excellent empire and was known far and wide for the fineness of his rule. He lived in his castle on the side of the hill. This kingdom had another hill on the other side of the river where the holy man lived. It was the duty of the holy man to teach, and the holy man held forth each morning to anyone who wanted to come and hear him.

He taught those great eternal truths which are the heritage of mankind, and which are meditated on by the holy men of society. So humble was the king, and so reverent of all things holy, that the king himself came over and sat among the listeners of the holy man. He asked no special place; he simply sat on the ground on a mat like everyone else. The holy man paid no more special attention to the king than to anyone else. This went on day after week after month, the king absorbing and appreciating the great wisdom of the holy man.

Among the listeners of the holy man, there was also a Sannyasin, a religious ascetic who has given up everything in the world and wears a yellow robe. This Sannyasin had practiced such renunciation that he needed only three things in the world: a begging bowl and two loincloths, one which he wore, and the other which was hanging on the wall to dry. For weeks and for months and for years, this small group of people sat and received the wisdom of the ages from the holy man.

Fate doesn't leave things static very long, and one day the Sannyasin went to the holy man and said, "I am fed up. Here I am, having renounced everything in the world. I have only a begging bowl and two loincloths, and you don't pay any more attention to me or give me any more honor than the king, who has renounced nothing. There's his palace over on the other hill, all of his harem, and all of his servants, and all of his gold and his fine food, and you treat him just as well as you treat me."

The holy man nodded, bowed, and said nothing. The Sannyasin was a little bit disappointed, but holy men do odd things and have a special timing of their own.

Sometimes when you ask a holy man something, you have to wait a while before he will answer, and sometimes he will answer in a way or a language or a timing that makes it some later moment before you realize you have been answered at all.

The next day, the group assembled to hear the words of the holy man. A messenger came quietly up, and whispered something into the ear of the king. The king nodded, and brought his attention back to the teaching of the holy man. A few minutes later, another messenger came up, in more urgency and haste, and whispered in a way all could hear that there was a forest fire near the palace, and that the palace was in danger. The king nodded, and listened to the further teachings of the holy man.

Yet another messenger came, and blurted out urgently, "The fire is getting closer to the palace, please come immediately."

The king nodded, and listened to the teachings of the holy man.

Yet another messenger came, and shouted across the group, "Your Highness, the fire is at the palace!"

The king nodded, and kept his attention on the holy man.

Another messenger came and said, "The fire has entered the palace and is burning irreparably parts of the palace grounds and the palace buildings."

The king nodded.

Yet another messenger came, and said, "The whole palace is on fire!"

No further messengers were needed, because one could look across the valley and see the palace enveloped in flames. The fire went on with lightning speed, and the whole palace was soon on fire, great billows of smoke rising into the sky. The king kept his attention on the teachings of the holy man.

The fire had soon consumed the entire palace, and was burning through the intervening forest, and was on its way to the place where the small group was assembled before the holy man. Soon they could smell the smoke, could hear the crackling of the fire, and soon they could even feel the heat of the fire. The king sat, listening carefully to the teachings of the holy man. He seemed to be oblivious to all of this.

Soon the fire was at the edge of the compound where they were, and was licking at the second loincloth of the Sannyasin, which was hanging on the wall to dry. The Sannyasin gave a yelp of anguish, jumped up, snatched his loincloth away from the oncoming fire, and patted the fire out of the cloth. Everything was instantly restored to its tranquility. The fire was gone, the palace sat in its serenity at the far side of the valley, the sun shone, and the breezes were cool and fine.

The Sannyasin, feeling terribly foolish, stood in the middle of things and looked at the holy man and said, "But what?"

And the holy man looked up and said, "Now, who is more attached to his property?"

Chapter 9
The Woman at the Crossroads
Introduced by Virginia Apperson

StarStruck, or maybe MoonStruck. That's what happened to me in my initial and in most encounters with Robert Johnson. He was the first Jungian elder in my life, and still stands out as a very singular one. More so than anyone I had previously met, Robert was enigmatically self-contained ... otherworldly. Maybe that's why I was almost always speechless in his presence. His quiet and gentle spirit invited a space for reflection, where words sometimes seemed superfluous. I guess because I felt a bit reserved around Robert, I didn't realize how much he had affected me. But his measure lives on, especially with regards to the utmost value he placed on conversing with the unconscious.

How many people in your life can you say truly model what it means to be in relationship to your most devilish and most diamond-like inner being? Robert lived it and held that gold for everyone that crossed his path, offering it up to be re-collected and integrated.

Here's one memorable exchange. He was leaving the Kanuga stage after giving a lecture, while I was approaching it for my very first Journey Into Wholeness presentation (a big deal for me). Uncharacteristically, he reached for my hand, put a piece of Citrine quartz in it (one of his treasures that he'd traded for in his precious second home, India) and said "Courage." I wear that stone on my right ring finger...a moxie-enhancing touchstone from one of my foremost teachers. In his generous and inimitable way, Robert made room for me and for many at the table.

And so, as Robert has taught me, I use active imagination to understand this story. I actively and imaginatively ask the Most Extraordinary and Valid Young Woman in this tale, the one who is true to herself and courageous enough to traverse the depths:

Virginia: What purpose does sitting at the Crossroads serve?

Woman: Each DIRECTION congregates here. Roads crisscross, touching one another within my soft core. My inhalations absorb the vital energy that comes from far afield, while my exhalations disseminate love, born from their quadrantal union. Planting myself in the crossroads emancipates me from a heavy, scripted lifestyle, enabling me to be solely accountable to myself.

Virginia: Okay, that helps me understand how immune you seem to people jeering and gawking at you, how oblivious you are to being ignored. Two gruesome extremes, being treated as a freak or invisible, and yet you are at peace.

Woman: That's right, Virginia. I get sustenance from wiser and more discerning witnesses. Investing in toxic energy is a ridiculous waste of my time and counter-intuitive to living a good life ... my life.

Virginia: The four ladies that showed up for you, they each offered their particular guises.

Woman: Yes, they did offer sweet consolation and congenial diversion, but more importantly they reminded me that I do not want a heavy, prescriptive load. And so I turn to what truly nourishes and substantiates me.

Virginia: What gives you the confidence to shed these conventional roles and bare your soul?

Woman: I love that question, it's actually an easy one. When we take the time to ask, listen, and look for the answer, we have a multitude of ratifying role models: Linger with a daffodil, a dandelion, or a chanterelle, each a marvel in their own right. They simply show up, as is, without a fuss, as they please.

A little sprout emerges, over time shape-shifting into its incomparable self. No sooner situated does Mother Nature then beckon her utterly unique children, each in their own wilting and drooping and decaying manner, to ebb towards the next season of being.

These are my tutors and mentors and companions. I remain in awe of how they remain stark naked, popping up and popping down in their own sweet time, a slow-motion balletic dance, arising and disintegrating to their own special, silent tune.

Yes, they're impacted by drought, Roundup, thunderstorms, and bulldozers. But in spite of it all, they are quintessentially born of the grandest matriarch of all, our Earth. And they rely primarily on living in their particular intersectional space.

They couldn't care less what others say or think or do. Light and simple, easy and subtle. A quiet, but radical revolution occurs sprout by bud by blossom, and so on, until time for wilt and rot.

Virginia: Goodness gracious! Just sitting in your presence, I can feel layers of stuff start to fall off of me, layers and layers. Your brazen lack of disguise makes me giddy and your conviction in a resourced vulnerability invites a trust and a confidence that I actually could dare to expose my truest self.

Woman: Yes, and can't you see Robert, with his Cheshire Cat grin, nodding with approval?

Virginia Apperson is a longtime searcher of conscious connections and found it in the writing of C.G. Jung and in the community of Journey Into Wholeness. With that foundation, she embarked on her Jungian analytic training at the C.G. Jung Institut in Kusnacht, Switzerland. Presently, she is in private practice in Atlanta, Georgia.

Once there was a woman, an extraordinary woman, and quite young. And for some strange reason, she sat herself down at the crossroads where the north, south, east, and west roads crossed. She sat herself down next to the crossroads stark naked. She sat there; various people objected, various people jeered at her, various people tried to help her, and most people ignored her. But eventually, a woman in gorgeous golden robes with pearls and diamonds sewn into patterns and ornaments came by, and took pity on the naked woman at the crossroads.

She said, "Here, you take this, you need it more than I do."

The naked woman looked at it and said, "But it's so heavy!"

And the woman of the golden robe said, "Yes, it is heavy, but that's not the worst of it. If you put on this robe, you have to agree to do what your wealthy husband tells you to do, and you have to be a showpiece for him. He will show you off, he will show all of his wealth off, by way of the wonderful clothing which you wear, and you may not make decisions of your own. You must always be at the beck and call of your wealthy husband, and gauge everything you do on whether it reflects well on him."

The girl without clothing said, "No, that's much too heavy." She took the robe and she set it down beside her, and the woman who had worn the golden robes came and sat next to her coat with the naked girl. Some time passed, more people came and went, some people jeered, some people ignored, and some people gawked; it was just what you would expect.

A woman in a very plain grey dress came by, and she said, "I have taken pity on you, you poor naked thing. You don't have to lie there in the ignominious situation you're in. You don't have to be naked: here." She took off her plain grey dress and gave it to the naked woman.

The naked woman looked at it, and she said, "Yes, that's better than the big, heavy one with the pearls and diamonds on it, but it's still too heavy. Why is it heavy?" she hefted it in her hand and said, "This is too heavy for a woman to put on."

The woman who had taken off the grey dress said, "Well, if you wear that dress, you give up all of your freedom. You may never rest, you may never have a vacation, you won't have time to be sick, ever, you will never have any time of your own. You will be busy cooking and washing and diapering and managing and being the head of a household. But, it's a nice dress."

And the naked woman said, "No, I could never put on that much of a weight. That's too heavy. I'd rather be naked." They waited a while; the second woman also sat down next to her dress, and wouldn't go away.

In due time, another woman, a flashy, flamboyant woman in a very short, bright, brilliant red dress came by, and she said, "You poor thing, lying there naked, I will give you my dress. It's easy, see, it can slip on and off in an instant."

The naked woman hefted it in her hand and said, "It's very heavy. Why is it so heavy?"

The woman of the red dress said, "If you wear that dress, you have to be at the beck and call of any man who wants you, and your life will be a series of unknown men who don't stay."

So the naked woman said, "No way will I put that dress on." And they waited a while, and of course the third woman sat down by her own dress, and they waited.

Presently, a nun came by with her nun's habit on, and she saw the girl with no clothing and said, "Here, poor child, you may have my dress. It's a dress of safety."

So the naked girl took it and hefted it in her hand and said, "It's so heavy."

The nun said, "Yes, yes, it's true, it's heavy. Because you will serve many people, and you will console many people, and you will help to raise children, but you will never have children. You will help women who have husbands, but you will never have a husband, and never know the joy of being a human being." So the girl said no.

The nun put her dress down and sat beside it. A long time passed. More people came, more people went. And, finally, some odd kind of alchemy sprung up between the five women and they began to talk, and each was telling the story of her life. How great it was to live in a convent and be safe. How exciting it was to live in a brothel and have a whole succession of men coming and going, even if they always went.

And the householder said, "It's so fine to have your own children, but you don't have your own life. You spend all of your energy being the backbone of the household. It's good, but it's very lonely too."

The wealthy woman said, "It's such a joy to parade before the neighborhood, to show off the gowns of my wealthy husband, but it's always for him. All this is for his benefit or for his prestige. Nobody ever looks at me for *me*. And one of the most awful things about this, I forgot to tell you, is that you must never grow old. You must never lose your shape, or you must go through the agony of seeing the glint in your husband's eye as he looks for beauty elsewhere."

The four didn't know what to do. Something was percolating; energy was accumulating. Finally, inventive as women can be, they took the four costumes and cut them up, and created a kind of synthesis, so that there was a bit of each costume in each of four dresses. They put them on, and they paraded, and they were pleased. They talked, and they walked around the naked girl.

The naked girl said, "No way." She went to a new crossroads.

Chapter 10
Heaven's Emissary
Introduced by Frank Roth

The story Heaven's Emissary, when told by Robert Johnson, always had the excitement of the pop of a champagne cork flying through the air. The story is about the perception of time and how you can lose yourself when you have fallen in love with life. It is about spirituality, not the kind that allows you to transcend the world, but one that grounds you deeply in it. This was one of Robert's great teachings, which became integral in his memoir Balancing Heaven and Earth.

I met Robert the night before a week-long Jungian conference in the mountains of North Carolina. I was one of the many young men that, after a mystical experience, found their way to him. My world had been turned upside down by a dream, a vision that was All Heaven, No Earth.

Robert was to do for me what Carl Jung did for him. He got my feet on the ground when all I wanted to do was fly away. He saved my life. He saved my life with a story. Robert interpreted my vision (in Jungian terms, my "Big Dream") and told me what I was to do. More importantly, he told me what I was not to do. It was time for me to be still. I was to become nothing. This was anything but what a principal dancer from New York wants to hear. He instructed me to read all of Jung, to read lots of myth, to learn the language of the dream time, and to learn how to use the I Ching—which took many years. Robert was patient and exacting. He spoke with such a matter-of-factness about the inner world you sometimes had to wonder whether he was serious or not. He was deadly serious.

I was in his room later that week, on the night I first heard Robert tell this story, when he said, "Frank, beloved, this is your story."

No one had ever given me a story. No one had ever said the word beloved to me, and I felt shattered like a windshield. Robert used words that seemed like they were from an ancient language, which was why he was such a good storyteller.

Over the next few years as I read and studied, I would go on to memorize Heaven's Emissary so I could tell it too. As I read the story again for this book, I discovered that I had altered the tale quite a lot. I had merged parts of Robert's Big Dream about the Buddha, the dream that he had told Carl Jung, into the story that I told. I had turned and churned this story from what I knew about Robert's dream life into something of my own making. What you are about to read is the story how I heard it for the first time. I read it again hearing his voice in my head and my heart... then pop!

So, my dear unknown friends, this is Robert's story, Robert's dream, and his gift to you. Use it. Enjoy It. Transform your life with it. Who knows? You may become immediately enlightened.

Frank Roth is a licensed massage therapist living in Greenville, South Carolina. He was a staff body-worker for Journey Into Wholeness, where he became friends with Robert. Originally from New York, Frank was a principal dancer for the Erick Hawkins Dance Company.

Once, there was an Emissary from the Gods sojourning on the face of the Earth. Occasionally, the Gods send someone to Earth on a particular errand. They masquerade very well, go about their business, and then go back to heaven again. This man was relaxing on the face of the Earth and no one was paying any attention to him because he looked just like any other body. But there was a yogi who was sitting in meditation by the road, far gone in a trance. He was so still in that sense of being that birds had built a nest in his hair and bees had built a hive on his right shoulder. He paid attention to nothing, no one bothered him, he saw nothing that went by on the road, but he sensed the presence of the man from heaven as no one else had.

So he woke up, and he called the attention of the man from heaven and said, "Oh man from heaven, next time you are in heaven please ask how long before my liberation. I meditate with all of the zeal I can possibly bear, but tell me how long before I will be liberated."

The man from heaven said, "Yes, I will inquire. The next time I am on the face of the Earth, I will come and tell you."

So the man from heaven went on, and he found a young man dancing underneath a banyan tree. Now banyan trees are wonderful things. The tree grows up and a limb goes out, and a root comes down which becomes a new trunk, and more limbs go out and another aerial root comes down which becomes another trunk. After some years you can't even tell which was the original trunk. A single Banyan tree can cover acres and acres and acres of ground. This is where the holy men sit. The man from heaven was walking by, and saw the young man dancing with great joy under the banyan tree.

He was curious, so he called to the young man and asked, "What in the world are you dancing for?"

The young man said, "I am dancing for my liberation! The next time you're in heaven, will you ask how long before my liberation?"

The man from heaven said, "Yes, indeed I will."

Some years later, the man from heaven was once again sojourning on the face of the Earth, and, remembering his promise, he brought news to the ascetic. He was sitting in such rapt meditation that the birds had built an even larger nest in his hair and still the beehive was on his right shoulder.

The man from heaven said, "I have asked the gods how long until your liberation, and they have told me seven more incarnations and you will be free."

The man groaned and said, "Seven incarnations?! How can I bear it?" The man contained himself again and said, "Well, alright."

He drew a deep breath and put himself back into his asceticism and into his meditation. The birds flew back into their nest in his hair and the bees settled down again. He began the seven incarnations of quieting himself until finally enlightenment might come to him.

The man from heaven went on, and found that the young man was still dancing under the banyan tree.

Without stopping his dancing, he called to the man from heaven and said, "Did you ask how long before my liberation?"

The emissary from heaven said, "Yes, I remembered my promise, and I've asked in heaven. The verdict is that you will be liberated in as many incarnations as yon banyan tree has leaves."

The young man leaped for joy and said, "What? So soon?"

Then a thunderous voice was heard from heaven saying, "Thy liberation is this instant."

Chapter 11
The Rainmaker
Introduced by J. Pittman McGehee

I met Robert Johnson when I was 30 years old. I attended a lecture of his and literally followed him home. He became my analyst, teacher, and guide. He had more influence on my process and worldview than anyone.

"The Rainmaker" so expresses Robert's psycho/ spiritual worldview: the psyche has its own time, and inner work prepares one for when it is time to rain!

J. Pittman McGehee, D.D., is an Episcopal priest and Jungian analyst. He is the author of seven books, a poet and an essayist, and is in private practice in Austin, Texas.

Once, there was a village in China which was besieged by drought. They were going to be in very serious trouble, and probably die of famine, if rain did not come soon. So, they tried everything, all the local things that they knew, but no rain. Finally, they sent a messenger to beseech the Great Rainmaker.

The Great Rainmaker came, looked about the village, and said, "Please build me a hut of rice straw outside of the village. Give me five days of food and five days of water, and leave me alone, please."

The villagers did this quickly. The Rainmaker disappeared into his hut with his five days of food and his five days of water, and at the end of the fourth day, it rained.

The people were overjoyed because their village was saved! The rains had come just in time and the crops were preserved. They went to the hut and dragged the poor Rainmaker out, blinking after the darkness of his little straw hut. The villagers shouted their thanks upon him, and gave him his fee. In addition, they gave him everything else that they could. He had literally saved all of their lives.

The villagers all shouted at once, "What did you do?"

"What is this marvelous process?"

"What is your magic?"

"How did you make it rain?"

He replied, "Oh, you see, I was uneasy, disquieted, and out of sorts with myself when I arrived in your village. I knew I had to put myself straight before I could even think of attempting any ceremonies. I had not yet gotten to the ceremonies at all. I was only putting myself right inside."

Chapter 12
Transposed Heads
Introduced by Ruth Hill

I remember the first time I met Robert. It was 1987 or 1988. I was in my late 30s, starting a psychological death and dying process as my marriage was ending, leaving all that I had known. As a Southern woman, I was to be a gracious, extroverted hostess, doing good works and serving and supporting "my man." I did this well.

Robert was a foil and an enigma to me. Him: all straight lines, silent, still, just being; me: no straight lines anywhere, talking to fill the silence, busy, doing. Polar opposites. I circled him, squinty-eyed, with sidelong glances, puzzling. He, with only the barest impulse of an eyebrow raised at me.

But things changed. I not only listened to his bedtime stories, I began to have brief but powerful encounters with him. Two stand out for me.

The first was while standing in the dinner line at Kanuga. I was bemoaning the fact that I was attracted to unavailable, hermit men, those who had a hard time connecting with their feelings. He, in very few words, told me I was talking more about myself than the men I was projecting onto. I was looking in the wrong direction.

Secondly, I had portable altars available at the conferences and I often wore oversized milagro hearts on a cord around my neck. By this time, I was part of the staff and often stayed in Cabin 8 with the speakers. One day, as I was getting ready to go to the lecture, Robert stopped in my doorway. This was so surprising to me the only thing I could do was stand still. Without a word, he stepped into my room and turned the heart that had turned backwards around so that it faced forward.

Stunned, I said without thinking, "Robert, you are the only man brave enough to touch the back of my heart." At that, he quickly removed himself from the room, I think as surprised as I was.

The time came when Robert and I could sit together peacefully. He had modeled for me how to of claim my own "hermit monk," my own wisdom, my own capacity to just be, and to come home to my true nature, to the dynamic stillness inside.

Robert said that Transposed Heads was the best story he knew, and "a woman's story." The love triangle of Sita, Shridaman, and Nanda and the entwined triangle of head, heart, and body. A woman yearns to find a man who is wise and knows his own nature. Until she looks into her own mirror and deepens into knowing the fullness of who she really is, meddling and searching for the missing pieces in the outer world will create chaos. It takes a long time for a woman to know herself.

Ruth Hill is a Craniosacral therapist and Enneagram teacher in Asheville, North Carolina. She delights in the continuing journey into wholeness, and her three grandchildren who provide the food for her exploration.

This is the story of fair Sita. She of the black hair, the moon face, the slender neck, the great bosom, the slender waist, the great hips, and delicate feet. Doe eyed, slow-eyed, almond-eyed, lotus-eyed, Sita. She was the loveliest of all maids.

Though the story is about her, it begins with two young men, Nanda and Shridaman. Shridaman was a Brahmin. The son of a Brahmin, the grandson of a Brahmin. He was from a long, long lineage of Brahmins. Shridaman also looked like a Brahmin. He had a slender, thin, slightly scrawny body, under a great, wonderful head. His body took on the proportions of a bent cucumber, as if it were tired of having to carry that magnificent head around. Nanda, who was his bosom companion, was a goat herder. He had a small head, a nose like a goat, and a wonderfully strong, sleek body with a lucky calf mark on his chest. The two boys were inseparable companions and were in fact blood brothers. In India, this meant they were two who had mixed and exchanged their blood early in their life, which meant companionship and identity and devotion between those two for the rest of their lives. In essence, every Indian man is married twice—once to his blood brother, and then later to the woman who is his wife. Shridaman went about his Brahmin business, and used his great head at every turn of the way, while Nanda herded his goats and was all muscles. The two boys loved each other profoundly.

Shridaman had to go somewhere on Brahmin business, and Nanda discovered that he had to go in the same direction for his herding, so off they went. Of course, Nanda carried the luggage for them both because his body never tired, while Shridaman woke up each morning already tired. They traveled until noon when the heat of the day overtook them.

They sat by a stream, having their lunch and discoursing. Shridaman was carrying on about lofty things, and Nanda was joshing him and telling him he should take some notice of earthly things. One of them noticed that a girl of ravishing beauty, thinking herself unseen, was standing a little distance from the river about to make her midday absolutions. She took off all of her clothing, thinking she was alone, and with the most dainty and graceful steps made her way down to the water. With a grace that was awe-inspiring, she went through her ceremony, slipped from the water to dry herself, then clothed herself once more and walked away.

Shridaman, scandalized, said, "We shouldn't have watched."

Nanda replied, "Didn't you once say we have to take the hard knocks of life, so we should also take the gifts?"

So, the two boys continued to gaze after her from behind their small barricade. Shridaman was strangely silent after this, and soon it came time for the two of them to part ways. They each had their separate businesses, so they arranged to meet in the same spot three days hence.

Nanda arrived back first, and was sitting in the shade waiting for Shridaman to arrive. He saw, even from far away, that Shridaman was in one of his terrible moods. Shridaman, with all of that head power of his, was occasionally overcome by awful, gloomy moods. That rarely happened to simple-minded Nanda. He went to meet Shridaman to cheer him up, as only Nanda could.

"Shridaman, you're behaving with all the dignity of a monkey freshly fallen from a tree. What's the matter?"

Shridaman said, "I can't speak. Just go get the wood for a funeral pyre, that I might cool my anguish in the flames."

Nanda understood this flowery language, and said, "Well you must understand that if you're to be consumed by a funeral pyre, I must go with you. I couldn't bear to live on the face of this earth without you."

This startled, pleased, and shocked Shridaman, because those words had never been said between them, though they both knew it was true.

Nanda saw that he had an advantage, so he continued, "Alright, I will build the funeral pyre if you will tell me what is the matter."

Shridaman burst forth, "I have fallen in love so desperately with that fair maiden that I can't go on living. Go gather the wood."

Nanda said, "I know that girl, Shridaman. She's the fair Sita from the next village. I have also held her in my arms."

103

You would have to live in India to know what a blasphemous statement that was, as you can never even look at a marriageable girl in India. To have had her in your arms would shake the heavens themselves.

Nanda told him the story. Once a year there was a festival in the old Indian villages, the Enticement of the Sun. People got so fearful as the sun grew weaker approaching December 21st, that on that critical day they chose the fairest maiden to offer to the sun. They scoured the countryside for the strongest man to throw her up into the sky as high as possible as an offering to the sun. This kept the sun coming back. It had been Nanda chosen to toss Sita into the air, so it was quite true and fair that Nanda had held Sita in his arms, if only for an instant. This startled poor Shridaman so badly that he lost his focus on the funeral pyre and began weeping.

Nanda saw an advantage and said, "There is a far less drastic way to deal with this. Send me as an emissary to woo Sita for you."

For that was the custom in India. You would never, ever woo a girl directly. You have to send your best friend to extol your many virtues and convince her of what a good husband you would make.

Shridaman said, "Do I have any reason to think she'd accept me?"

And Nanda said, "Of course! You're the most eligible Brahmin bachelor in the area and you'd be the catch of the season. Sita's parents will do what they all do, refuse the first three offers and then agree to the fourth. It's as good as done. No more talk about funeral pyres."

So, Nanda went off and began the many months process of courting fair Sita for Shridaman. Finally, Nanda asked and was refused, asked and was refused, asked and was refused, and on the fourth offer, they consented to have Shridaman as son-in-law. An astrologer had to be employed, and permission had to be granted from Shridaman's parents. One set of parents had to visit the other, and some months had to go by before the other set could visit the first. Finally, the astrologer found a suitable date, and the marriage took place.

After the marriage, the couple were not allowed to lay eyes on each other until after the first five days. They were not allowed to have seen each other before the marriage either. After the five days of festivities, a kind of endurance contest, the groom led the bride seven times around the camphor fire at the altar. They were both so heavily bedecked with flowers that neither could see the other. Then they were pronounced man and wife and the flowers were removed. But here is the awful thing, the dreadful thing. It was then that Sita saw her husband for the first time, but he saw her for the second. No good could come from this and it did not bode well for their future.

They lived happily, and of course Nanda stayed with Shridaman. They could not possibly live without the other. So, they made a household in Shridaman's parents' house, and a terrible thing happened. Fair Sita, virtuous and noble as she was, found that she couldn't keep her eyes off the sleek, wonderful body of Nanda. In monastic terminology, she lost custody of her eyes, and her eyes wandered to the powerful and beautiful body of Nanda every time she forgot herself. Sita had an awful anguish inside of her because of this, and Nanda was extremely uncomfortable because he couldn't help but notice. Shridaman remained oblivious.

Whenever anything is going wrong, the first thing one does is hasten to reassure everyone in sight that things are going perfectly. This is true all over the world. So, they all decided to go to Sita's parents and tell them of the child on the way to show how well the marriage was going. Everybody was relieved at this idea, and it broke the tension of their complicated household. Nanda hitched up the cart, Shridaman and Sita sat in the back, and off they went. It's a rule, perfectly well known to everybody, that if you're lost inside, you'll become lost outside very quickly. Nanda made a wrong turn somewhere along the way, and the road dwindled before them until it was only a footpath, and soon it wasn't even that. Night fell around them and they were lost.

They had a terrible night in the cart. The mosquitos were awful, the three of them were at odds with each other, and there was no peace. At dawn, Shridaman saw that they were very close to a Kali temple. Kali is the darkest of the female gods. She has eighteen arms, wolf's teeth, blood coming from her mouth, snakes for hair, and each of her eighteen arms holds something more terrible and horrible than the last. One holds a skull, another holds a snake, another has some bones, one has entrails, and so it goes. Kali is the goddess of destruction.

Shridaman said, "Give me just five minutes to go and pray to Kali, and then we will continue on."

He went in and faced the terrible visage of Kali, which defeated him. He was heartbroken for he had finally seen their horrible situation. In a terrible spasm of despair, he took the knife from his side and severed his own head.

In his last words he said, "The least I can do on this earth is add my own blood to the worship of Kali."

Sita and Nanda were sitting outside alone, terribly distraught and uncomfortable. Finally, Sita could stand it no longer.

"Nanda, go get that good for nothing husband of mine. He's probably fallen into one of his trances and he'll be there until noon."

Nanda went in and saw the ruin of his life, because without Shridaman he couldn't bear to live. Without thought and without decision, he grabbed the knife from the still quivering body of his beloved Shridaman and severed his own head, adding his blood to the sacrifice to Kali.

Sita sat there for five more minutes, getting into quite the temper.

She said, "Those two have probably gotten into a theological debate. They've forgotten all about me and I'm being eaten up by mosquitos."

So she went in and there she was met by the ruin of her own life. Her beloved husband dead, along with her beloved Nanda. She staggered out of the temple, waited a moment, and looked back in to see if it was all just a terrible nightmare. There were the two bodies, and there were the two heads. She was wrapping a vine around her neck to hang herself when a loud, gruff voice issued forth from the temple and called her name.

It was the goddess Kali, coming down from her pedestal.

She walked out, and said, "Sita, you are guilty of such a terrible crime that your punishment is even worse than death. You must live. Besides, another life is at stake too."

Poor Sita burst into tears and threw herself at the feet of the goddess, and her entreaties were so profound and so deep that even the heart of Kali was touched.

Kali said, "Alright, if you truly do repent of what you have done, because it is your fault the two are dead, you may go in and perform a miracle. Put the heads back on the bodies and the two will live."

Sita went in and, only half believing, took one of the heads by the hair and put it on the body of Shridaman. Immediately the miracle happened, and the body quickened into life and Shridaman stood up. She took the other head by the hair, and being careful to face it frontwards, put it on the other body, which also quickened and stood up.

The three ran outside and were dancing in a circle for the renewal of life. But then Shridaman was confused as he stroked his wonderfully sleek, muscular body with the lucky calf mark on his chest. Nanda was wondering what had happened to him as he gazed at the thin, emaciated little body which was underneath him. For you see, Sita had transposed the heads. The noble head was on the noble body and the goat-nosed head sat on the inadequate body. Sita, to her great disgrace, laughed.

An argument immediately broke forth, and Shridaman with Nanda's body reached out to touch Sita, and

Nanda with Shridaman's body shrieked, "You may not put your hands on my wife."

Shridaman says, "But it's I who said the marriage vows!"

Nanda replies, "But it's my body who conceived the child with her."

The two of them found themselves deadlocked in the only disagreement they had had in their life. Who was Sita married to? Shridaman with Nanda's body, or Nanda with Shridaman's? When such a thing happens in India, you have to take it to the nearest great, holy man. There was a famous holy man three days' journey away in the forest of Dancaca. They hitched up the cart, and there was another tussle as to who was to sit beside Sita and who was to drive the cart. But Nanda's body was the only one strong enough to carry the cart, so Nanda, who knew the way but lacked the strength, told Shridaman how to manage and off they went.

They arrived and asked for the holy man, but the people wouldn't let just anyone talk to their holy man, lest he be pestered to death. Sita explained the situation, and one of the wives of an attendant was so intrigued that for the promise of knowing what the holy man said, she told them how to find him. It seemed that Nanda, feeling so dreadfully inferior, had come to the holy man before and the holy man had told him that he was to do austerities to calm that big body of his down and become more spiritual.

When the holy man saw Nanda coming with Shridaman's body, he said, "Ah ha! I see the austerity has worked very well! You are very thin and ascetic looking."

But Nanda with Shridaman's body didn't say much to that, so the holy man asked, "Or is there something else?"

Nanda said, "Yes, indeed there is something else," and poured out the whole story.

The holy man said, "You unenlightened people can get yourselves into the worst situations ever and I don't know what to do about this. I have to meditate. Give me three days."

They came back in three days' time. The holy man decreed that since the word is more powerful than the act, he who said the vows is the true husband of Sita. Shridaman with Nanda's body was the true husband of Sita, and Nanda with Shridaman's body was to take up residence under a banyan tree in a neighboring village and live as an ascetic. Shridaman with Nanda's body hitched up the cart, and they went back. Shridaman with Nanda's body was terrified, because he would not be recognizable with his great, strong body and the lucky calf mark on his chest.

He went straight to his parents, and from some distance his mother clapped her hands and said, "See! I said you need only to get married and you would prosper! You have filled out, and I have never seen you so fine!"

Some months went by, the baby was born, and Sita was terrified. She got up from the birth bed as quickly as she could, because there's a long tradition in India that if a wife conceives a child, thinking of someone else, the child will be born blind. But the child was quite fine. Things seemed to be going well, but Sita, to her horror, discovered that the Brahmin head of Shridaman began destroying the muscles of the Nanda body. Before many months were over, it was once again Shridaman's body with its little bent cucumber form.

Sita guessed that Nanda with Shridaman's body, because of the dominance of the head, must have grown sleek and muscly with the lucky calf mark on his chest again. She had to go and see him. One night she took Samadhi, their son, and hitched up the cart long before dawn and left. By dawn, Shridaman with Nanda's body, who knew what was going to happen, arrived at the forest of Dancaca after following Sita. He saw a scene which was painful beyond description, but was one he had expected. He saw a hut in which Nanda with Shridaman's body, now grown sleek and powerful, was lying in a romantic embrace with his beloved Sita. Shridaman went to the river Ganges a short distance away and stood in meditation, nowhere now for him to go.

When Nanda and Sita woke, they went to the river for their morning ablutions and saw Shridaman standing there. The three of them stood together in silence. Each of them knew, without words, that any happiness in the world which is gained at the unhappiness of someone else, any brightness that is the darkness of another, or any advantage which works at the disadvantage of another, is not worth it. Just by the meeting of eyes, the three knew they must construct a funeral pyre.

Nanda, with Shridaman's body, went off to collect wood for the funeral pyre of three. Fair Sita, she of the black hair, the moon face, the slender neck, the great bosom, the slender waist, the great hips, and delicate feet, ascended the pyre. Doe eyed, slow-eyed, almond-eyed, lotus-eyed, Sita, sat down in the center. Shridaman, with Nanda's body, ascended the pyre and sat on Sita's right. Nanda, with Shridaman's body, ascended and sat at Sita's left. Samadhi, who was only just old enough to do the sacred rights of the oldest living male relative, took a stick and lit the pyre. So intense were the three upon their intention, that not a sound escaped their lips as the pyre consumed them. The pyre burnt for the required 24 hours, before the ashes and bones were swept into the Ganges river.

Samadhi was given to one of the temple widows to be raised. At the age of twelve, he was taken to the Brahmins and taught. As you would expect, he had a wonderful, fine Brahmin's head, a strong and vigorous body, and an absolutely distinct lucky calf mark on his chest. At age 21, he was given into the service of the Maharaja of Benares, as his reader, and became a famous and brilliant scholar in his lifetime.

Chapter 13
The Old Jew
Introduced by Jim Cullipher

My wife, Annette, and I met Robert Johnson in the early 1980s, the fledgling years of Journey Into Wholeness. We traveled to California to work with John (Jack) Sanford on our dreams, and he suggested an analyst for each of us. Robert was selected for me.

At that time, Robert was preparing for one of his first international speaking events with Marie Louise von Franz. Jack invited us to join a group of their friends that were gathering to watch a trial run of his lecture. Poor Robert was a bundle of nerves and the lecture was a disaster! His friends advised him not to speak like someone he wasn't. His feeling function would carry him if he let it, and he shouldn't try to "lecture" in a way that wasn't natural. Robert went back and completely revised his talk and, apparently, was a huge hit. Jack tried to convince us to invite Robert to speak at our events, but we were a little wary after witnessing this first attempt. We finally agreed, and Robert spoke at our conferences every year for over 20 years after that. Jack was right.

In addition to being our most regular lecturer, Robert was our dear friend. He impacted our lives, and those of the Journey community, in countless ways. Robert and Annette had an active correspondence for years and this was a great gift in her life. We visited him, he stayed with us before all of our events, and we traveled together when our events took us out of the country. He was our family.

As well as being a wise man and a powerful presence, Robert also had a keen sense of humor. He loved a funny story and his delivery was masterful. The Old Jew is an excellent example of his funnier side.

Jim Cullipher worked as a research chemist in the atomic energy field before serving as an Episcopal priest in churches in Tennessee, Florida, and South Carolina. He co-founded Journey Into Wholeness with his late wife, Annette, and organized events on depth psychology and spirituality for 30 years.

Once, there was an old Jew who lived in a small city. Life had not been good to him. He was penniless and he lived in the poorest section of town, but then an even greater disaster fell upon him. He simply couldn't bear it.

He sought out his friend, Ami, and said, "Ami, I have to tell you something. I raised my only son a good Jew, but then he went out into the world and came home a Christian. What did I do wrong?"

Ami was silent for quite a while and then said, "It's strange you should mention it, because my only son has also come home a Christian. I haven't had the strength to tell anyone, and I am so humiliated."

The two sat there a while and finally said, "Well, we have to go to Rahm, the rich man. He will know what to do."

So they went to Rahm, the wealthy man, and they poured out their misery on him.

Rahm, the wealthy man, said, "So strange you should mention it. My only son has also come back a Christian, and I haven't had the courage to tell the Jewish community. What did I do wrong? Why don't we seek wisdom from the rabbi?"

They went to the rabbi, and they poured out their agony on him, and he was silent for quite a while.

"Strange you should mention it. I, of all people, the rabbi of this town, should not have a son that returned a Christian. But I do. We must go and ask Yaweh directly."

So, they called to Yaweh, besought him, and laid all of their collective sorrow out to him. There was a great silence from the heavens for a very long time.

Finally, Yaweh replied, "Strange you should mention it."

Milton Keynes UK
Ingram Content Group UK Ltd.
UKHW011309290424
441932UK00011B/31/J